AU

AND HOW TO FIND IT

A pom's musings on the Great South land

Patsy Trench

Prefab Publications

Contents

Update 2020

Since this book went to publication in late 2019 eastern Australia has suffered its worst bushfires ever. They dominated the news here in the UK, and elsewhere, for weeks, rendering my passing comment on how Australia rarely features in our news channels obsolete. Now the whole world knows a whole lot more about the great south land, including, and especially, who Scott Morrison (aka Sco-Mo) is, and his and his party's views on climate change.

I was following the fires through various news channels on social media and elsewhere, including direct experiences from friends who were evacuated or forced to stay indoors in raging heat because of smoke pollution. The essence of what I learned is contained in a Postscript. Hopefully it will not need to be updated any time soon.

Prologue

The family historian

She sits alone, in her kitchen, or her bedroom, or maybe even in her office. Just her, a computer, a desk and a pile of books. Shoulders ludicrously hunched, nose almost touching the screen, as if her breath alone can conjure magic out of those search engines. If she's lucky she'll have a relatively unusual surname, though thanks to the traditional family habit of naming their offspring after themselves she'll have a merry time figuring out James senior from James junior and James junior junior. She spends a good deal of time sighing, and occasionally swearing and muttering to herself, and wondering whose idea it was in the first place to set off down this endless, foggy path into her family history.

It doesn't help to know it was her idea, and that no one ever forced her to do this, or pressured her to keep going, or let's face it, gives a hoot one way or another.

The one thing she knows is she will never give up: despite the outside world's indifference, the loneliness and the frustration and the thought of all those other things she could usefully be doing with her life, such as earning a living, or volunteering, or improving her house. This is not a hobby, it is an addiction.

On occasion, as a treat, she will don her hat and gloves and trot into town to visit the library. This is a real day out: lofty surroundings, special, even rare books, carefully selected and placed reverentially on the desk in front of her.

Hours later and they're switching off the lights and metaphorically putting the chairs on the tables. She blinks into the daylight and forces herself with difficulty back into the 21st century. It's not until she gets home and looks through her notes that she realises, really, how little of value she's managed to discover in all that time. Except. *Except.* You never know. Nothing is ever wasted, except time.

Now and again the miraculous happens. After hours rummaging through Trove[1], hunting, hunting, revising the search terms, ignoring the creeping feelings of despair, the ticking clock and the rumble of a stomach deprived of nourishment, she has a Eureka moment: a genuine find, a nugget of new information, a solution to a mystery only she was ever aware of. This is her very own piece of solid gold. So what if her excitement is out of all proportion to the size of the piece of the jigsaw. It is one small step on the way to the filling in of the puzzle, the lifting of the fog.

From time to time she will receive a message from a stranger, a distant relative who's found her on the internet. And they will share their knowledge and findings, and the puzzle will become a little more complete and for a short glorious moment she will know she is not alone.

She is in her own way a hero. Unsung, unrecognized, but a hero nonetheless.

Introduction

So what's this all about?

Back in 2007 I was at a bit of a loss. My marriage had broken down and my part-time job, where I'd been working for three years – a record for me – wasn't doing much for me any more. So I decided to make a complete break. I gave up the job, let out my flat in London and went to Australia to research my family history.

I kept a diary at the time, always a useful thing to do. I called it *The left hand side of the escalator*, which is a reference to one of many differences between the Aussies and the Brits. While we both drive on the left hand side of the road, for reasons unknown we in England stand on the right hand side of escalators and Aussies on the left. These things being so automatic I realised that when I began to spontaneously take up position on the left in Australia I'd been there long enough to become, if not quite an Aussie, at least temporarily acclimatised.

Reading back through the diary I see I was terrified at the prospect of giving up job and home to fly off to a country where I had neither of those things, on a whim, with no financial backing. I had never let a property before, and to make things worse with a week to go before my flight the various letting agents I'd contacted still had not found me a tenant.

However there was a quote that kept reverberating in my brain and spurred me on, namely:

> 'Sometimes the fear of the unknown is not as great as the fear of things staying the way they are.' (Richard Price, *he Paris Review Interviews*)

I was in my early sixties then and I was beginning to be aware of the passing of the years and the dwindling opportunities available to someone of that age. It was a now or never time, you could say. I had no idea if the plan would work, whether I'd find enough of interest to turn into a book, whether I was capable of writing a book set in a different time and largely in a different country, whether or not I'd end up penniless or homeless and the whole enterprise showed itself to be a waste of time.

It turned out to be one of the best decisions I've ever made. It opened out for me a whole new world of family history and it gave me the courage to know it is possible to step out into something completely new at that age. I became an *aficionado*, if not an addict, of family history and of Australian colonial history in particular. Anyone who's delved into their family background even lightly knows how easy it is to get immediately and all-consumingly caught up in the lives of their ancestors, to the detriment of all other preoccupations and duties, domestic and otherwise.

And exactly five days before I was due to fly I found tenants for my flat.

♈

My mother was Australian, though you'd never know it. She came to England in her early twenties to study at RADA (the Royal Academy of Dramatic Art), and since in those days there was only one acceptable accent for anyone wanting to make a career in the acting business – known then as the King's English and now as RP, or

Received Pronunciation – the first thing she had to do was get rid of her Australian accent, which she did with one hundred percent success.

I tried hard not to be like my mother, but I somehow found myself repeating her experiences almost exactly, only in reverse. At the age of 23 I turned back the wheel she had set in motion and migrated from my home in England to Australia, at a time when the Australian government paid people to do such a thing. We were called ten pound poms, as that is how much it cost us to fly there. I stayed in Australia for three years before the homesickness got to me and I came home again.

I've made several visits to the great south land more recently, if only to escape the British winter, during which I got chatting to my Australian aunt Barbara. Of three sisters born there she was the only one who remained in Australia, and she had spent her retirement years looking into our family history going back to the 16th century and beyond. I discovered on my mother's side that we were descended from King Edward I via his daughter Joan of Acre, sister to Edward II (as are many others if they care to look).

But more specifically I learned about my original Australian pioneer ancestress Mary Matcham Pitt, my four times great-grandmother, a widow, who at the age of 52 left her home in the village of Fiddleford in Dorset along with her five children to make a new home in a penal colony in what was then known as New South Wales. It was 1801, not that long ago by the standards of the Plantagenets but very early days so far as colonial New South Wales was concerned. What had started out as a penal colony was then barely thirteen years old, and of around 5000 Europeans living there fewer than 40 of them were free settlers.

Needless to say my ears were seriously pricking up

13

now. If I had had trepidations about packing up my home and making what was a relatively easy journey across the world to a country I had been to before, knowing I would be coming home again, what must it have been like for my g-g-g-g-grandmother to be doing the same, only to a penal colony few people had ever visited or knew anything about, knowing she would never see her homeland again? Not to mention the six month sea voyage on a convict ship.

Well, there was certainly a story there.

It took me six years, but I eventually wrote and published Mary's adventures in a book I called *The Worst Country in the World*. This was followed six years later by *A Country To Be Reckoned With,* about Mary's grandson GM, pioneer farmer, local dignitary and founder of the stock and station agent Pitt, Son & Badgery. During that time I've flown back and forth between England and Australia countless times, I've travelled through most of countryside New South Wales and visited every library I could find in search of stories not only to do with my ancestors, but about the country itself, its history and its history wars. Oh and along the way I've been granted dual Anglo-Australian citizenship due to a change in the law that includes the immediate offspring of people born in Australia. I can now work in Australia, own property there, open a bank account and enter the country without a visa or restriction of any kind. Hoorah.

So this book is a miscellany of odds and sods I picked up on the way, mostly to do with Australia past and present, and how the world views it, then and now, with my own observations thrown in. There are little-known anecdotes about Admiral Nelson and quotes from the likes of Anthony Trollope and Mark Twain. There's a chapter on Sydney's beach bathing by-laws and a pom's take on the Aboriginal community, as it concerned my own family and beyond. All of it is written from the point of view of the outsider researching her family history from afar and the astonishing discoveries she made along the way about a country, a family, and herself.

Chapter 1

What is the purpose of family history?

> 'A people without the knowledge of their past history, origin and culture is like a tree without roots.' Marcus Garvey

There are myriad reasons behind the family history addiction, as I call it. While we are all naturally curious about where we came from and who we think we are, my motivation stemmed from an emerging fascination with the context of my ancestors' lives. The reason I decided to write about my ancestress was because she was one of the earliest free settlers to migrate to New South Wales. It was the story behind her migration, and behind the colonisation of that far-flung country in the first place, that grabbed me.

Family history, broadly speaking, is about ordinary people. Traditional historians tend to focus on the famous, the ones in the foreground of the picture so to speak. Family historians are more likely to be looking at the people in the background, whom nobody outside the immediate family has heard of. That doesn't make them unimportant, or boring. It's the ordinary people who keep the wheels of everyday life turning. Our ancestors needn't have done anything remarkable to make them worth writing about.

In the blurbs of the two books I've written about my family I rather grandly claim I'm 'looking at Australian colonial history through the lives of my [fill in appropriate ancestor/ancestress].' I am unwittingly taking on the role of historian, and perhaps wittingly trying to avoid the term family history because who is going to read a book about my family except, well, my family? It wasn't just because I wanted to sell more books that I broadened my sight lines; it was because I genuinely believe history told through the eyes of ordinary people is every bit as valid, and revealing, as history told about the heroes and the luminaries.

> 'There are only two lasting bequests we can
> hope to give our children. One of these is roots;
> the other, wings.' Hodding S. Carter

There are other more important things to be gained from investigating your family history of course, and, more to the point, sharing it with your kids. It gives them, according to psychiatric reports, a sense of identity and belonging. Children who know something of where they come from have a greater sense of self-esteem and resilience, so it's said.[1]

Personally speaking I haven't yet managed to interest my offspring that much in their family background, but if and when they do want to know about it I have a couple of books to set them on their way. After all it took me the best part of sixty years to become interested in my family history, well after both my parents had died. If I say it is a massive shame they weren't still around then I can only remind myself of those fifty odd years when they were.

> 'Why waste your money looking up your
> family tree? Just go into politics and your
> opponents will do it for you.' Mark Twain

Haha. Or, if you are a celebrity, the BBC's *Who do you think you are* will do the work for you. In the case of actor Danny Dyer, of *Eastenders* fame, you will discover you are descended from King Edward III and before him, William the Conqueror. What effect that has on you depends on you of course. Dyer, the original working class lad done good, born and bred in the East End and who now lives in a beautiful house and drives an SUV, was rendered speechless. What part his family heritage played in what looks like a highly successful professional and private life (knowing nothing about him other than how he appears on that TV programme) – well, who knows?

I too am descended from King Edward III through my paternal grandmother, and his father Edward II through my maternal grandmother (does that make my family inbred?); as are tens of thousands of us if you go back far enough. My parents were what you would call upper middle class, living in Chelsea and at one point Belgravia, Conservative-voting, comfortably off rather than wealthy – the properties we lived in were leased rather than owned. To outward eyes I've come down in the world, living as I do in a two bedroom flat in unfashionable Dollis Hill in north London (and I own the freehold). And I've never voted Conservative in my life and don't ever intend to. But I am also descended from convicts transported to Australia for, respectively, being in possession of forged banknotes and theft. I don't feel I truly identify with any of my ancestors, ancient or modern, royal or criminal. But then isn't that the crux of the whole family history business? We are a bit of everyone who came before us, a link in a long chain, but in the end we are ourselves and not really like any of them.

To quote Ralph Waldo Emerson:

> 'Every man is a quotation from all his ancestors.'

Chapter 2

Australia and how to find it

February 2020: In light of the recent bushfires, which have placed Australia in headline news around the world, please see my postscript.

In 1855, at the height of the goldrush in Victoria, a man named Henry Capper produced a pamphlet, price 6d, entitled *The Australian Colonies: where they are, and how to get to them.*

He advised readers to buy a map, 'look at the right hand lower corner, and there will be seen a very large island – the largest in the world – this is Australia, or as it was called in former days, New Holland . . . New South Wales [which] can be found on the east coast, or right hand side of the map, is larger than the kingdom of Portugal.'

He described the general layout of the continent, its weather ('seasons are reversed'), its topography ('If it is allowed that only one half of Australia is good land, that will yet be twelve times as large as the whole of England, Scotland and Ireland'), its wildlife, including snakes ('not many, few venomous') and insects ('mosquitoes and ants numerous and troublesome'), and in particular – bearing in mind his expected readership – the fact that the country, especially Victoria and New South Wales, was rich in minerals.

Apart from the snakes his description was remarkably accurate. He also outlined the type of person who might be eligible for 'assisted migration', viz: 'The industrious, sober, healthy of the following classes: female servants, bakers, butchers, brickmakers, bricklayers . . . The class of person not wanted . . . are clerks, shop men, artists, schoolmasters, lawyers, doctors, workmen in the finer arts . . .' unless they were prepared to work as labourers. Likewise for the women: 'governesses, milliners, dressmakers, and any females who are not of the *labouring* classes are not wanted'. This explains why virtually all my Australian antecedents, with the notable exceptions of my pioneer Australian emigrée Mary Pitt, and my good self, were 'unassisted migrants': they did not pursue 'useful' professions.[2]

Most 21st century Europeans probably have a rough idea where Australia is, but the country still rarely features in British consciousness, except when it comes to sport, and cricket in particular. This is partly because it is by and large a peaceful place that is not trying to extricate itself from a complex partnership with its neighbours, is not governed by a xenophobic racist, is not currently suffering from famine or civil war, and has never been invaded – except by the Europeans back in 1788 of course.

In 2018 Australia ranked third in the United Nations' Human Development Report (which takes into account life expectancy, education, and income per capita), below Norway and Switzerland but above every other country.[3] Globally it ranks below Canada in influence and power. Australians took part in the Vietnam War, which the British did not, and later the Iraq War, which the British also did. Why? That's not for me to say. But there was a story going around at the time that when Vice President of the US Dick Cheney visited Sydney and was told the Australians were thinking of withdrawing their troops from Iraq (500 of them I believe), he effectively said, 'So what?'

When I first arrived in Sydney way back in 1968 I was struck by the similarities of day-to-day stuff such as milk bottles, library systems and the sense of humour. It took me longer, oddly enough, to clock the huge differences in climate, and in language. Australians have their own unique language, some of which – such as 'whinge, 'a big ask', 'footie', 'no worries' and so on – have been adopted here in England too. Geographically the country resembles the US far more than the UK, and they have adopted Americanisms such as 'pants' for trousers, and the habit of asking you how you are rhetorically. They call starters 'entrées'. They are fond of 'verbing' nouns – as in 'farewelling' dead people and 'euthanasing' injured animals – and they love acronyms. They pronounce the word 'router' (aka modem) like the Americans do, as in 'rowter'. If you go into a computer shop, as I did, and ask for a router as in rooter you will get funny looks. The word root, in Australia, has a quite different meaning. For example: 'What is the definition of a wombat? A creature who eats, roots and leaves.' (If you're not Australian you won't get the joke.) They call sparkling wine champagne without blinking an eye and accuse you of snobbishness if you protest.

They have electric sockets in bathrooms and think nothing of plugging in heaters right next to the hand basin. Their food is varied and luscious and their pharmaceuticals are expensive. They conserve water better than us (they have to) and complain about the cost of petrol, which is half the price it is here in the UK but then they drive ten times further. Their public transport is, put politely, idiosyncratic.

Australians themselves are generally open, exceptionally friendly, sometimes brash and foul-mouthed, and have a predilection for chintz. They call their bric-a-brac 'antiques'. They are sophisticated, suburban, multi-cultural, xenophobic (just like us), patriotic and proud to admit it (not like us). Contrary to popular myth they are largely law-abiding and conservative. They are classless, up to a point, yet they are fascinated by our royal family and they are not yet a republic. They are suspicious of intellectuals and they despise 'tall poppies', as we do but for different reasons: it breaks the Aussie code of 'all mates together' to be that much richer or more successful than your everyday bloke in the street.

These comments needless to say are drawn from personal experience over the years rather than anything approaching empirical research.

The Australian male by and large prefers the company of other males to females, which is why at a social gathering it is not unusual to see the two sexes congregating in different parts of the room. He can also wear his emotions surprisingly near the surface, as I witnessed a few years ago.

It was Valentine's Day and I was having dinner with a female friend in a restaurant in the Sydney suburb of Coogee, when a couple sat down at the table next to us clutching a 'Happy Valentine's Day' balloon. He was a fair bit older than her, in his mid-forties probably, and she was Scandinavian and in her twenties. He started to chat to us and discovered we were friends through our respective offspring, who at the time were going out together, which he thought was really nice. He told us he had split up with his wife and had walked out leaving her and the kid and the house, and he was now living in a hotel. His new (we assumed) girlfriend was smiley and sweet and didn't seem to mind too much that her boyfriend, on Valentine's Day, was spending most of the evening talking to two middle-aged women.

Then my friend happened to say something like, 'It must be tough leaving your son behind like that', and without warning the man burst into tears. It only lasted half a minute, and he then recovered and carried on as if nothing had happened.

On another occasion I was listening to the radio one afternoon in Sydney and they were discussing an interview they'd broadcast earlier in the day with a farmer, talking about the drought, which was the worst in living memory. How moving it was, they said, the pride he had in his land and in his country; his positive attitude, his good humour, his poetry.

I eventually heard the interview. The farmer was bluff, friendly, casual and wry, and yes, he did become quite poetic, especially when describing the effect a bad drought has on the earth. Droughts he said were necessary for the well-being of the soil: when a drought causes the earth to crack and form fissures, the rain when it does fall penetrates right through to nourish the soil well below the surface (a theory a farmer friend later debunked completely by the way, which makes the radio farmer's unwavering optimism all the more remarkable). What impressed the people in the studio was the farmer's almost matter-of-fact attitude of acceptance, his good-humoured determination to see the best in everything and his overwhelming love for his land. And then people started calling in, listeners who had heard the interview, and I heard more than one of them saying: 'It makes me proud to be Australian.'

Australians celebrate tradition far more than we do. Anzac Day, which falls on April 25th every year and is a part-public holiday, and which commemorates the part played by Australians and New Zealanders in the various wars and Gallipoli in World War 1 in particular (hence the date), is a major event, with dawn services held in cities and towns throughout the country. Then there's Australia Day, on January 26th, which celebrates the arrival of the First Fleet into Port Jackson (aka Sydney Harbour) in 1788. The Queen's official birthday in June is a public holiday.

Someone, I don't remember who but probably a politician, once suggested in *The Guardian* that we have a 'British Day' to celebrate being British. The response was robust. 'British Day? What on earth do we have to celebrate? There is no such thing as Britishness,' protested the letter writers. And even if there were it would be tasteless and jingoistic to celebrate it, they went on. We do of course have St George's Day on 23 April (coincidentally the birth and death date of William Shakespeare), but that tends to slip by unnoticed. Not so Scottish Burns' night and Irish St Patrick's Day.

That's what I mean about patriotism. I don't believe Australians are necessarily any more patriotic than the Brits, it's just they're less inhibited about it and more inclined to express it out loud.

When it comes to their government, it looks to me to be even more at odds with its people than ours. The current incumbents do not recognise climate change, and have done some pretty brutal things to asylum seekers. The Australian Liberal government, which at the time of writing has been in power since 2013 (in 2019 they won an election against all the predictions) is somewhat to the right of our current Conservative party, and the extreme right wing in Australia is closer to the seat of government than ours.[4] Populist, xenophobic radio 'shock jocks' have big followings. But then we have the Daily Mail and Nigel Farage.

At the same time parts of Australia I've visited are way ahead of us when it comes to renewable energy and recycling schemes, and the people I spoke to were incandescent at some of the recent anti-muslim comments emitting from right wing politicians (this in the wake of the terrorist atrocity in Christchurch, New Zealand). The image Australia sometimes has of a regressive (they were one of the last western countries to legalise same-sex marriage), isolationist (they give less in foreign aid than many poorer countries), racist country is partly true. But, again, it all depends on who you talk to.

Personal experience you understand. Of course our friends think much as we do, that is why they are our friends.

Back in 2007, Nicholas Stern, the British economist, was visiting Australia to speak to the powers that be – at that time the Liberal Party under John Howard – about climate change. He told them, as he had told us a few months before in the UK, that if we didn't drastically change our ways in the next decade we would experience an economic depression worse than we could ever imagine. He wasn't necessarily giving us any new facts about the environment, he was talking about the effect on our pockets.

The powers that be (in Australia) said get lost, it is impossible to cut carbon emissions without drastically threatening our economy and causing massive redundancies in our coal industry, which is considerably larger than yours. And moreover, if the USA isn't going to sign the Kyoto agreement, not to mention India and China, then why should we? One or two commentators added: Who do you think you are, coming over here and telling us what to do? We're not bloody colonials any longer, matey. And so the leader of the country of Australia, which was then in the throes of the most horrendous drought – the worst since Federation, 100 years earlier, so bad that every four days a farmer killed himself – gave the two-finger salute to climate change.

Then a week later there was something called 'Earth Day', where for one hour on Saturday night, from 7.30 to 8.30pm, the residents and commercial businesses of Sydney were invited to turn off all their lights and other electrical equipment as a gesture towards climate change. And so for an hour the city was plunged into darkness, apart from the street lights, and the savings on energy were huge and everyone rejoiced. Earth hour has spread to other parts of the world now, but as far as I know it originated in Australia.

More recently, there is the Adani coalmine, the size of Britain, owned by Indians but located in Queensland. A subject of much discussion and dispute, it was given the official go-ahead earlier this year, albeit on a smaller scale than originally planned.

Then three months later, on the recent global Climate Strike Day on 19 September 2019 Australia's young people led the world by taking to the city streets in their hundreds of thousands marching in support of action on climate change.

So it's hard to know who or what really represents Australia.

Culturally Australia is not recognised as being in the top rank – not because the country lacks culture, but because so much of the best of it doesn't travel, simply because it is uniquely Australian. And whereas Aussies will happily sit in front of quintessentially British exports such as *Dad's Army* or *Fawlty Tow*ers – or even, God help us, *Midsomer Murders* – the Australian equivalent rarely seems to hit our television screens. And whose fault is that?

One of the most memorable live shows I have ever

seen, still in my consciousness fifty years later, was *The Legend of King O'Malley* – a gloriously irreverent take-off of the man, an American as it happened, who 'created Canberra'. More recently there was *'Keating!'*, an equally hilarious piss-take of the rise and fall of the ex Labor prime minister. To my knowledge neither of these shows has been produced outside Australia. *The Boy from Oz*, a musical based on Peter Allen, singer-songwriter and, briefly, husband of Liza Minelli, ran on Broadway but never reached London. Tim Winton's *Cloudstreet* had a brief run at the National Theatre here in London (which I missed because the performance I booked for was cancelled – due, I later learned from my Australian brother, to the fact that the leading actor had broken his ankle in a cricket match between the cast and the British crew). The Sydney Theatre Company's miraculous *The Secret River*, adapted by playwright Andrew Bovell and director Neil Armfield from Kate Grenville's Booker Prize-nominated book – which I saw in a quarry near Adelaide two years ago, one of the most memorable nights I've ever spent at the theatre – has recently enjoyed a brief spell here in London at our National Theatre, to rave reviews and standing ovations, demonstrating that the Brits are not wholly indifferent to Australian history. But it took six years to get here and was only on for just over two weeks. The ABC television series of the same book has yet to be shown here.

Talking of which – when did you last see an Australian production on prime time British TV? BBC4 a while ago showed a well-made and highly topical 6-part series about a clash between well-to-do Brisbanites and a sinking boat of asylum seekers called *Safe Harbour*. Yet the landmark series of recent years, *Redfern Now*, which tells separate stories of Aboriginal families living in a suburb of Sydney, has not yet appeared on our terrestrial channels, and why not? (It is available on Netflix, watch it if you can.) Meanwhile *Banished*, the BBC series about the arrival of the First Fleet in 1788, notable for its total lack of Aboriginal characters, and like *Redfern Now* the brainchild of Liverpool's Jimmy McGovern, was shown on BBC2 and dismissed out of hand by critics at both ends of the globe. It never made it to a second series as a result. Australian commercial channels show more ads more often than all of us combined have had hot dinners, and yet there is a TV channel, SBS, dedicated entirely to European and Asian programmes, which is more than we have.

Ali G, aka Sacha Baron Cohen – famous in the UK and the US – was not the first dim-witted character to conduct straight-faced mock interviews with famous people. Norman Gunston, aka actor Garry McDonald, was doing exactly that back in the 1970s. (Clips of his shows can be seen on YouTube.) Nor was *Twenty Twelve*, the much-loved BBC 'mockumentary' about the lead-up to the Olympics, a British invention. The Aussies did it twelve years earlier, with *The Games,* which was not aired on British TV, needless to say. The makers of *The Games* not surprisingly accused the BBC of plagiarism, which they, not surprisingly, denied. Co-creator and lead actor (the late) John Clarke described himself on his website as running 'a charitable institute supplying formats to British television'.[5]

Literary-wise, if I can use such a word, Australia punches way above its weight. The image the country often has of a sports-crazy, outdoor-world fanatic, anti-intellectual nation is not the full picture. If Australian books, paintings, films and plays do not feature much in British consciousness there is only one nation that is to blame, and it isn't Australia. Australia is a much more inventive, interesting, and above all *different* place than many Brits realise.

Chapter 3

Colonisation

In 2007 I attended a seminar on the History Wars at the New South Wales Writers' Centre in Rozelle, Sydney, where for the first time I witnessed what I came to realise is the customary opening announcement at any public event, namely: 'We acknowledge the [name of Aboriginal group], the traditional owners of this land.' I found this bemusing, perhaps tokenistic, but would never dare say as much out loud.

The well-known Tasmanian historian Henry Reynolds was on the panel and he has written extensively on the history wars. Roughly speaking they refer to the ever changing perception of Australian colonial history, according to where you are on the political spectrum and whoever is running the country at the time. In 2007 it was Liberal Prime Minister John Howard, who for whatever reason refused for all the time he was in office, despite a good deal of pressure, to say Sorry to the Aboriginal people whose land, and at one time whose children, the colonials had purloined. His successor, Labor's Kevin Rudd, endeared himself to the whole country (if briefly) by devoting his inaugural speech to doing just that. (I was there at the time, watching it live on TV, it was a very moving moment.) Also on the panel of the all-day seminar was the Aboriginal writer Ruby Langford Ginibi, who I remember partly for her wryly-delivered joke: 'What is the definition of an Aboriginal family? Mother, father, two kids and an anthropologist.'

Although I am a pom I appreciate I am implicated in the history wars because the first three generations of my ancestors received land grants, which effectively means they stole the land from the local people. So I should feel guilty. On the other hand those same pioneers endured tremendous hardship and deprivation, and showed great fortitude and enterprise in the course of turning what to western eyes was an untamed country (the worst country in the world) into what they considered habitable (a country to be reckoned with). So I can feel proud.

Yet again, it is complicated.

∞

If you compare the beginnings of the colonisation of the US and Australia – and can set aside for the moment the rights and wrongs of such a thing in the first place – the Australian record is pretty impressive.

The first Englishmen to set foot on American soil went there for commercial reasons, with private funding, and for the first ten or fifteen years roughly 80% of them perished. 170 years later the government-organised First Fleet landed in New South Wales with 1000 or so convicts on board and enough provisions to last them two years. When two and a half years went by without a whisper from the old country it looked as if the colony might starve to death, and you could say if it hadn't been for the resourceful and fiercely disciplined Governor Phillip that's exactly what would have happened.

In both cases the newcomers depended very much on the local inhabitants, who taught them how to fish, how to understand local weather conditions, how to find their way about, and so on. In both cases those same inhabitants became less friendly the more they realised the interlopers intended to stay, to steal their land and as far as possible to wipe them out.

Nowadays it is not considered appropriate to celebrate the arrival of the Europeans and the devastating effect this had on a local people who'd lived on the continent for upwards of 60,000 years. Australia Day, the annual holiday commemorating the arrival of the First Fleet, has connotations, and there are strong movements afoot to change the date to something more inclusive, and reconciliatory.

Watch, as the saying goes, this space.

φ

A few years ago a group of enterprising antipodeans organised a Festival of Australian and New Zealand Literature and Arts at King's College in London. It ran for two or three years before, presumably, the funding ran out.

The second festival, in 2015, took place at the same time as an exhibition running at the British Museum called *Indigenous Australia*, and the focus of the first talk I attended, called 'Who owns culture?' was whether or not an institution such as the British Museum had the right to hang onto artefacts acquired from elsewhere, often in dubious circumstances.

On the panel, along with the curator of the exhibition, an anthropologist who had been working in Vanuatu and the chairperson, journalist Tim Radford, was Aboriginal writer Melissa Lucashenko. She was a feisty lady who liked not to mince her words, and her opening salvo was along the lines of: 'You took our land and our children, and now our artefacts, and we want them back.' She even went so far as to say that the exhibition was wasted on the Brits, judging by conversations she had picked up on.

They didn't understand the exhibits or their significance, and the exhibition did nothing to further their knowledge of Aboriginal history.

As we know from the Elgin Marbles the British Museum does not give up its acquisitions easily. Repatriation is governed by complex legislation apparently, and each case is different. For example it took twenty years of negotiation – from 1986 to 2006 – to return a set of human remains from the British Museum to its origins in Tasmania. That, it seems, was Ms Lucashenko's point, that it was the essence of colonialism to assume that the rights of an institution like the British Museum exceeded the rights of Aboriginal people. An exhibitor had a 'moral obligation' to return artefacts after an exhibition is over, she maintained. Besides, the Aboriginal people needed them if they were going to prove Native Title.

Native Title recognises that 'Indigenous people have rights and interests to their land that come from their traditional laws and customs.' (Native Title Act, 1993). But it is very limited, apparently. The first claim was turned down because, according to the judge, 'The tide of history has washed away your entitlements.' Oral evidence was not recognised, hence the added importance of the artefacts.

When asked if the Australian government would help with repatriation Ms Lucashenko replied that the current government – Liberal, and headed by Tony Abbott – would like all Aboriginal people to disappear off the face of the earth.

I had to confess I began to see the whole affair in a different light. Many of the exhibits of *Indigenous Australia* had apparently been in storage in the bowels of the British Museum before the exhibition opened and presumably would be returned there after it closed, for however long, out of sight and mind.

But what shocked me more than anything was my own part in all of this. As a born and bred Londoner I have spent my lifetime enjoying the astonishing range of what this crowded, difficult city has to offer in its museums and galleries, without giving a thought to whether they had the right to display those offerings in the first place. I like to think I am an enlightened person, but perhaps I too am guilty of a latent sense of entitlement.

The next talk was called 'The indigenous voice'. On the panel were Aboriginal writer Tony Birch and Australian author Kate Grenville, and the topic for discussion was, effectively, 'Who has the right to write about Aboriginal matters?'

Kate Grenville confessed the reason Aboriginal characters were largely absent from her bestselling novel *The Secret River* was because as a white writer she did not feel she could properly represent them. 'Our lot had taken everything from the Aboriginal people', she said. 'So to try to tell the story from their point of view would be the last insult.'

If a white writer cannot write about Australia's original inhabitants does that mean they don't exist? Could colonial guilt lead to what Tony Birch called 'the danger of silence', when a nation is too ashamed to talk about the atrocities committed in its past, and therefore resorts to saying nothing at all? 'It is the public secret we all know' but don't talk about, he said. The suppression of these stories – of any story other than the 'official' one – was a sign of 'an insecure country.'

Once again I found myself confused, and implicated. As a pom I felt doubly unqualified to feature Aboriginal people in my books as anything other than peripheral characters. In *The Worst Country in the World* I took a leaf out of Kate Grenville's book and virtually avoided featuring any Aboriginal people at all. There is one (invented) scene when an Aboriginal man turns up on my ancestor's property – or what he assumes to be his property – on the Hawkesbury River, begging for food. It was there to illustrate the awful irony, of which in my account my ancestor was fully aware, of a people who had been self-sufficient for upwards of 60,000 years being forced to beg food off the very people who were taking their means of self-sufficiency from them. It was there to demonstrate the enlightenment I had granted to my g-g-g-grandfather, and of course my own.

It's a thorny topic, to say the least. I had always assumed a writer could write from the point of view of anyone of any age, sex and from any period. Kate Grenville's central character was a 19th century London-born male convict. She is a 20th century Australian-born woman. Besides, writers in the recent past, notably Thomas Keneally in *The Chant of Jimmy Blacksmith* and Eleanor Dark with her *Timeless Land* trilogy, had no such qualms.

But perceptions change, as I learned from my introduction to Australia's history wars. Whether that sensitivity, or self-imposed censorship, adds to general reconciliation and mutual understanding between whites and blacks is another matter.

ထ

A few years ago in the midst of my researches for my second book (*A Country To Be Reckoned With*) I was contacted by an Aboriginal man called, for the purpose of this narrative, Martin Pitt claiming we were related.[1] Martin was born in Moree, in northwest New South Wales, where he told me there are hundreds of Aboriginal Pitts still living, all of whom appear to be descended from a Tom Pitt, who was born in 1848. Tom Pitt not being an Aboriginal name it was Martin's guess his ancestor acquired his name from my great great grandfather

George Matcham Pitt (subject of *A Country*), who happened to be in Moree at the time of Tom Pitt's birth in 1848, 'taking up' land.

Excited? I was. And still am. It was fairly regular practice I'm told for Aboriginal people to take the name of white people back in the 19th century, often their employer's, partly for protection and partly to make it easier for white people to identify them. This of course does not mean Martin and I are blood relatives – not unless my g-g-grandfather was up to no good, which I would half like to believe but in reality don't. But it is intriguing nonetheless to think I have a near-direct link with the Kamilaroi people of northern New South Wales.

I researched Tom Pitt as far as I could, with Martin's help. I posted a request in the local paper, the *Moree Champion*, asking for any Aboriginal Pitts to contact me. Several did, though I never did get to meet with any of them while I was in Australia, regretfully. When I got back home I started up a discussion on a Facebook group, which is when I hit the buffers.

Aboriginal history, I was firmly told, belongs to Aboriginal people. White people who try to write about it are regarded with great suspicion. No matter how often I tried to reassure my correspondents that I was only interested in the name connection and how it may have come about, I was effectively told to go away and mind my own business.

 I was annoyed, needless to say, and rather hurt. But I was then told by an enlightened (white) Australian friend that there is still a huge gulf in understanding and trust between Aboriginal people and the white usurpers of Australia. While I maintained from the start I would never presume to write about Aboriginal history except in collaboration with an Aboriginal person, I am still not welcome. Australian history is too often told from a white point of view. White Australian historians glean their information from records created by white people. Aboriginal history is passed down orally through the generations. The two are not compatible. And as far as I can see at this particular moment, they never will be.

So be it.

∞

As a postscript to this chapter, I would like to relate a story concerning whites and blacks that appeared in my first book, *The Worst Country in the World.*

In 1839 the Legislative Council of colonial New South Wales sent a questionnaire to all pastoralists asking for feedback on the usefulness or otherwise of any Aboriginal labourers they employed on their land.[2]

In answer to the question - How could the 'Native Blacks' be induced to work harder – one respondent replied:

> 'By cutting off their great toes. They could not then climb the trees for opossums. Two hours so spent or in fishing will supply them with all they want for the day; why then should they vex themselves with the drudgery of labour? They are not fools . . .'

As for their prevailing character:

> 'They are not labourers at all, and for the same reason that any other gentleman is not, viz that he can live without labour . . . They realise the philosophy that Diogenes only dreamt of, yet are no Cynics, rather Gymnosophists. But surely the Council will not encourage a 'degraded class' among our pure population.'[3]

The Council clerk's handwritten response, scribbled on the front page, went, 'As it conveys rather more insult to the Committee than information, I shall be authorised to exclude from those selected for publication.'

Chapter 4

Horatio and George

Why am I writing about Horatio Nelson?
The link is a man named George Matcham. He was my ancestress Mary Pitt's first cousin, and he was married to Nelson's youngest sister Catherine, known as Kitty in the family. It was George who was responsible, with the help of the Nelson name, for initiating and arranging Mary's migration to New South Wales.

It's always exciting for a family historian to find a connection to a famous name, and it takes a good deal of discipline not to get carried away by it, a discipline I did not have. I read up everything I could about Nelson in the course of my research, too much if truth be known, as while his name and position may have been influential when it came to my family being granted land in New South Wales, he was never the central focus of my story.

In the course of my research I came upon a wonderful book called *The Nelsons of Burnham Thorpe*, written by George's great-granddaughter Mary Eyre Matcham. It contains some fascinating snippets about the Matcham and Nelson families, some of which I touched on in my first book, *The Worst Country in the World*. So here is an opportunity to pass on some of the less relevant yet no less intriguing facts about that famous man.

Horatio and George were great friends as well as brothers-in-law. George had been left a healthy inheritance at a young age at the death of his father and often helped out with the Nelson family's finances. He was friends too with Nelson's father, the Reverend Edmund, who had brought up his children single-handed after the death of his wife when Horatio was only three years old. The book is compiled mostly from letters written between various members of the Nelson and Matcham families, and in particular between Edmund and Kitty; and after the Reverend's death, from diaries kept by George's eldest son, George Matcham junior.

Horatio was born with two useful assets: courage and charisma. As a child at school he escaped from the dormitory window one night, using sheets, in order to steal pears from 'a dreaded schoolteacher' who had a fondness for flogging. He gave the pears to his schoolmates, keeping none for himself, and when a prize of five guineas was offered 'to discover the plunderer' no one said a word, as 'Nelson was too much beloved for any boy to betray him.'[4] He volunteered for the navy at twelve years old in order, according to *TNOBT*, to relieve his father of the strain of his upkeep.

We all know that Nelson lost first an eye, and then an arm, in the course of his naval duties. He was shot in the head at the Battle of Calvi in 1793, causing 'a gaping hole' above his right eye, and was discharged after a month's treatment by the ship's surgeon. Four years later during the Battle of Santa Cruz a ball from a musket passed through his arm, causing it to be amputated. According to one story he was back issuing orders to his men half an hour later,[5] though it appears from Ms Eyre Matcham's book that it took him a good six months to recover completely.

Nelson's bravery was never in doubt, but what's almost as remarkable is how he was able to make a joke of both these calamities.

After he lost his eye Horatio was refused a pension until he could produce a formal certificate to prove it. When he later lost his arm, after a moment of 'vexation' he began to see the funny side and insisted on the surgeon providing him with another certificate to verify the loss of that, 'which he declared might just as well be doubted as the other.' So he drew up a petition on behalf of his remaining left arm. The letter, dictated by Nelson, written by his brother William and sister Catherine and signed by Nelson himself as 'Nelson's left hand', is reproduced in *TNOBT* and goes like this:

> 'To THE NURSES, PARENTS & GUARDIANS OF THE KINGDOMS OF GREAT BRITAIN & IRELAND
>
> '. . . Whereas your humble Petitioner has had the mis-fortune to lose his Brother in His Majesty's Service, & is now obliged to do all his Master's work himself, to which he is by no means competent. This is to certify in behalf of himself & the whole race, that they have been from time immemorial, greatly abridged of their Just rights & Privileges.
>
> 'They therefore respectfully submit to your consideration the following observations & humbly hope that you will condescend to take Notice of their lamentable case.
>
> 'And first, no person has ever endeavoured to insinuate that right hands were made before left; so that no peculiar privilege can be claimed by either party, on the score of seniority.
>
> 'Secondly, the left hand is as long & strong

by Nature as the right, has as many joints, fingers & nails; wherefore no Just title to pre-eminence can be asserted by either, founded upon superior capability.

'For these reasons, we would have an equitable, true & perfect equality to be established between us according to the laws of Reason & Nature: & neither of us to be superior or inferior to the other.

'Instead of which, you must acknowledge that at present, We the left hands have been kept in a state of comparative ignorance, & barbarism.

'This arises solely from our want of education, for while the favoured right hand is attended by the very best masters in writing, drawing, & fencing &c. the poor left hand is neglected, forgotten & hangs aukwardly [sic] dangling by the side; except now and then when called in to assist in some drudgery which the right hand does not choose to do by himself. Barbarous custom too has excluded us from a participation of the most pleasant offices that our nature is capable of; if we meet our friends & acquaintances, we are not suffered to move, but the right hands instantly leap to embrace each other & enjoy the delight of friendship. How often has your petitioner itched to take a Lady by the hand, but yet never was permitted, tho' the right was engaged in all the offices of Gallantry, and in battle, when my noble Master, God bless him, was hewing down the Dons with the right hand, your petitioner remained unemployed, liable to all the injuries of war without the

40

means of defence or retaliation.

'. . . Should his arguments have any weight with You & the prayer of his humble petition be taken into consideration & produce a change of system, Your petitioner will together with all his fellow sufferers be bound in Your service by the strong ties of gratitude & your petitioners shall ever pray.

'Admiral Nelson's left hand.'

Nelson is almost as well known for his private life as for his achievements at sea, and needless to say his domestic carryings-on caused considerable embarrassment within the family. He had a wife, called Fanny, with whom he had no children. (She had a son from her first marriage, but for some reason she and Horatio did not produce any more.) Fanny spent a lot of her time alone while her husband was at sea, much of it with her father-in-law Edmund.

It seems the Nelsons and Matchams tolerated Fanny rather than liked her. She had a habit of complaining, and she was described, by the likeable Kitty, as 'rather cold'. Even the kindly Edmund found her presence irksome from time to time. On one occasion when the Nelsons were visiting him he archly remarked: 'Mrs N takes large doses of the Bed; and finds herself only comfortable when enclosed in Moreen.'[6]

Still, Fanny did not have an easy life coping without her husband. And as we all know after several years of marriage Nelson abandoned her for the infamous Emma, Lady Hamilton, and their affair was conducted with the full knowledge, even approval, of Emma's husband Sir William, to the extent that the three of them lived together in what became known as a '*tria juncta in uno*'. But when Nelson and the Hamiltons fetched up in England family loyalties were stretched to the extreme. Fanny, poor, neglected, complaining Fanny, was pretty well side-lined by everyone except the gentle Reverend, who struggled to reconcile himself to his son's behaviour. When Nelson arrived in London in 1800 with Emma and her husband in tow he virtually ignored Fanny and humiliated her in public. And when George and Kitty were invited to spend the Christmas of 1801 with the Nelsons at Merton they declined, possibly because without the mediating presence of Edmund they were too embarrassed at Horatio's treatment of his wife.

Emma was a beautiful, ambitious and flamboyant woman with a colourful history. She had been deposited on Sir William in Naples, where he was British Ambassador, by his nephew, who was also Emma's lover and anxious to get rid of her so he could marry someone else. Sir William, who was thirty-five years older than Emma, took her under his wing and eventually married her. Emma had been an artist's model, and she had an illegitimate child she'd been forced to give away for adoption. Sir William was genuinely fond of Emma, but as time went on he began to find her flamboyance and occasionally hysterical behaviour exhausting, so when Nelson arrived on the scene he was very happy to hand her over to him; and even on one occasion when the admiral was absent Sir William wrote to him begging him to return, so he could have a break from Emma. As Sir William grew older he recognised that Nelson loved Emma in a way he never could, and while the affair caused him considerable grief, and damage to his pride and reputation, he liked and relied on Nelson too much to try to stop it.[7]

In the film *The Nelson Affair*, adapted from Terence Rattigan's play *A Bequest to the Nation* and in which the Horatio/Emma story is viewed through the priggish, outraged eyes of George Matcham junior, Emma is played, by Glenda Jackson, as a foul-mouthed harridan. Whether or not this was a true representation her letters to Kitty Matcham show her to be warm to the point of gushing, yet always and totally devoted to her lover.

Nelson and Emma had a child, named Horatia, whom they kept very secret. She was handed over a few days after her birth to a Mrs Gibson to bring up, and up until his death Horatio referred to her in public as his 'adopted' daughter. Privately however he set up a trust for Horatia, which he handed to her 'protector and guardian' Emma, along with a letter addressed to Horatia herself acknowledging her as his child.[8] Just before he died Nelson added a codicil to his will asking that Emma should be given a pension of £500 a year by the state, which was ignored. After his death Emma got into terrible debt, mostly due to her extravagance. She spent time in a debtors' prison and had to be bailed out by friends, and finally to escape her creditors she fled to Calais with Horatia, where, two years later, she died, still in poverty.

So my immediate thought was – where was George in all of this? Why did he and Kitty not come to Emma's aid? It seems Kitty did in fact offer to have Horatia come to live with them, and to pay Emma enough to cover her household debts, but Emma did not want to let go of Horatia – who, incidentally, had no idea Emma was her mother. In a letter to his son before Emma left for France George had written to say, 'Lady Hamilton has been harassed and grievously insulted by her creditors.' He also did his best to mediate in quarrels that developed between Emma and some of her former staff. So it seems the Matchams did not neglect Emma.

Horatia finally did go to live with George and Kitty Matcham after Emma's death, though whether or not they told her who her mother was I've no idea. Thankfully Nelson and Emma's daughter went on to marry and have children and live a long and, let's hope, a happy life.

ϙ

Later in his life, in a book published privately for his family, George Matcham paid tribute to his late brother-in-law. Nelson was, said George:

> 'Of a delicate structure, of a reflective mind, strongly tinged with melancholy, retired and domestic in his habits . . . As he had contempt for bodily ease or comfort, so he had a total & heroic disregard of danger. He went a willing victim to his country's safety and renown, and seemed from the moment that he entered on his profession, to devote his life to this great end, with the firm belief . . . that he was to breathe his last in the arms of victory under the British flag.
>
> ' . . . Little versed in the mean arts of lesser man, and wholly unacquainted with worldliness . . . Lauded, admired, and sought everywhere but at home, where complaining and reproach formed a sad contrast to the merited reception he met with elsewhere, he naturally turned from the spot, his heart sickened and revolted, and was at last completely estranged.
>
> '. . . His warm heart eagerly strove to attach itself to some object of primary affection: if Lady Hamilton had not artfully endeavoured to inveigle it, some other female would. . .
>
> 'But Lady H.'s disposition was satirical, not I believe from malignity of disposition or temper, but from an affectation of point and wit. Her letters and even casual notes were never free from this despicable propensity. Lord N. in reply to her, could not but

somewhat flatteringly adopt her style; that he ever did an act, to the prejudice of another, we may defy the whole world to prove . . . with gentle manners, and of a temper never ruffled, but of unparalleled sweetness, he was the delight of every house he blessed with his company.'

So there we have it. Nothing about Horatio's private life, in George's eyes, could tarnish him. It was his wife's fault for giving him a hard time at home that caused him to look for solace and love elsewhere. And if he ever adopted a mocking tone – what I assume George meant by 'satirical' – it was because he picked up the habit from Emma.

Nelson was courageous, clever, vain, and a superstar in the eyes of the public. It would have been a tough task, after the open adulation he received everywhere he went, for the poor woman left at home to live up to it. That said, there is nothing to excuse the way he deliberately humiliated his wife by flaunting his lover in front of her in public.

The exotic yet adoring Emma was obviously far better suited as Nelson's companion and lover than his lacklustre wife. She fed his vanity, she entertained him and outraged him. How could loyal, retiring, unflamboyant Fanny compete with that?

∞

The name of Nelson, Duke of Bronte, is ubiquitous in Australia. The suburb of Bronte, in Sydney, on Nelson Bay, is named after him, as is Bronte House. Bronte is a surprisingly common forename in Australia, for women rather than men. More specifically in my family's case, one of the first grants given to my ancestress on the Hawkesbury was named Nelson Farm, and later the two adjoining properties acquired the name of Bronte, a name

45

which exists to this day. There's also a Bronte Park in Tasmania named after the admiral by George and Kitty's son in law Captain Arthur Davies, who married their daughter Elizabeth and migrated there in 1828.

Precisely how much influence the Nelson name had on the achievements of Mary and her family is hard to gauge – it's tempting for the family historian to exaggerate when it comes to famous connections. The early governors of New South Wales were all naval men, and no name would have held higher esteem for Governor King – who, it's said, hosted the Pitt family on their arrival in the colony. Mary arrived with a letter of recommendation from the Reverend Nelson, and she was given grants soon after arriving in New South Wales, but then so were her fellow settlers.

Who knows?

As for me, despite his messy private life I am happy to claim Nelson as my cousin-in-law seven times removed.

Chapter 5

Dickens, Trollope and Twain

When I was researching my possible Aboriginal antecedents I came upon a first-hand account of a trial at Maitland Assizes of an Aboriginal man named 'The Duke of Wellington'. It appeared in a British weekly journal called *Household Words,* written, or so I thought, by none other than Charles Dickens.

Wellington was a friend of another Aboriginal man called 'Fryingpan', who appeared in the dock with him, accused of spearing a cow on a property belonging to my great-great-grandfather. Fryingpan's trial was postponed to a later date, but Wellington's went ahead and the report appeared in Dickens' journal under the title *Going Circuit at the Antipodes*.

It was both a hilarious and disturbing account of a man completely out of his depth. Wellington appeared to find the trial proceedings highly amusing, and when he set eyes on the judge in his full regalia he burst out laughing and invited the rest of the court to join him, which despite themselves they did. Notwithstanding the hilarity Wellington was convicted of the crime and taken away, still smiling, to face a sentence of ten years' transportation from his home and his family, and almost certain early death.

The writer was appalled to witness this 'poor child of nature' – whose name, and Fryingpan's, was probably bestowed on him by merry-making convicts – being mocked and put through the wringer in such an alien environment as an English court. The empathy and concern in the piece sounded pure Dickens to me, but it wasn't until I probed a little further that I learned the writer was not Dickens but a visiting English lawyer called Archibald Michie. *Household Words* was 'conducted', or edited, by Dickens and the articles were published anonymously, though Dickens took an active part in the editing process and apparently rewrote many of the contributions.[1]

So another hopeful, if distant, family connection with a famous person was dashed. Dickens never set foot in Australia himself, although he sent two of his sons there, neither of whom appeared to thrive.

∞

Anthony Trollope's son also went to live in Australia, at the age of eighteen and probably of his own volition. Unlike Dickens Trollope spent over a year in the great south land in 1881-2, travelling through all six colonies and writing about everything from the climate to animal welfare, convict history to the Aboriginal people. His earlier writings appeared in serial form in the British *Daily Telegraph*, and the final result was published in three volumes of over 1,000 pages under the title *Australia and New Zealand.* Trollope was the first major 'celebrity' to visit the country from overseas and his presence was, according to the *Brisbane Courier,* 'as carefully watched and recorded by the press as a royal progress.'[2]

Trollope loved Australia, and Sydney in particular, which he grew so fond of he felt tearful on leaving it; though he couldn't resist taking the Mickey out of its bewildering fortifications, which included armed fortresses, torpedoes and a boom placed across the harbour to keep "them" out. Who "they" were, he was not able to establish.

He praised the standards of education throughout the colonies, particularly in country areas. He reported on the fact that the labouring man in Australia earned twice as much as his British counterpart, and ate meat three times a day to his poorer colleague's none. He was bemused by the preoccupation with owning mineral shares, and he was critical of the divorce laws, which 'alone among English-speaking races' did not exist.

Above all he was impressed with life in the bush, in which he spent some time, with his son and with others, and the strange hierarchy that had evolved among the pastoralists:

> 'The number of sheep at these stations will generally indicate with fair accuracy the mode of life at the head station. A hundred thousand sheep and upwards require a professed man-cook and a butler to look after them; forty thousand sheep cannot be shorn without a piano; twenty thousand is the lowest number that renders napkins at dinner imperative. Ten thousand require absolute plenty, meat in plenty, tea in plenty, brandy and water and colonial wine in plenty, but do not expect champagne, sherry, or made dishes . . .'[3]

Trollope's *Daily Telegraph* series was syndicated to newspapers in Australia, and the Queensland press in particular did not like what he said. They even questioned the right of anyone who had not lived in the country for several years to pass judgment in the first place. Ignoring Trollope's complimentary comments on the friendliness and informality of Queenslanders *The Brisbane Courier* homed in on his criticisms of cruel farming practices. As they foresaw he would do, Trollope had written 'about Australia and things Australian hastily and without experience.'[4]

They did not appear to complain so much about Trollope's comments on the 'disagreeable subject' of the Aboriginal people. He described their marriage laws, their corroborees and their skill at tracking men and cattle as 'very wonderful'; but they had made no progress for centuries, and the arrival of the white man, rather than civilising them, had led them to adopt the worst of their vices – such as drunkenness and thieving – and none of their virtues. At the same time he also questioned the settlers' right to take the country from its original owners, though he didn't think the Dutch or the French would have done any differently.

'Of the Australian black man we may certainly say that he has to go,' he asserted. But 'That he should perish without unnecessary suffering should be the aim of all who are concerned in the matter.'[5]

In Trollope's defence this was the prevailing view at the time apparently, and his comments about 'unnecessary suffering' were considered progressive.

But the biggest blot on Trollope's copybook was his reference to the Australian partiality for what he called 'blowing':

> 'You're told constantly that colonial meat and colonial wine, colonial fruit and colonial flour, colonial horses and colonial sport, are better than any meat, wine, fruit, flour, horses, or sport to be found elsewhere . . . Now if I was sending a young man to the Australian colonies, the last word of advice I should give him would be against this practice. "Don't blow," – I should say to him.'[6]

Visitors to Australia in the past, including myself, often

joke about how before their feet have barely touched the tarmac of the airport someone is popping up in front of them to ask, 'What do you think of our country?'

It was part of what used to be called the 'cultural cringe' – a term coined in Australia to describe the mixture of inferiority and defensiveness specific to a country that does not yet believe in itself or its people. When I was living there in the late '60s and '70s it was taken for granted, particularly in my world of the arts and entertainment, that a person had to go abroad to make his or her name. Henry Lawson bemoaned the fact that the highest praise a poet could achieve in his home country was to be called 'the Australian Kipling' or 'Australian Southey' etc; as if the country could not produce its own top-ranking poets, artists and actors who didn't have to be constantly compared with their equivalents in the Old Country. I experienced a bit of this myself. I even benefited from it. When I first arrived in Australia the very fact that I was English gave me a positive advantage when it came to finding acting work. But I could feel the tide turning while I was there, helped along by locally-made, globally-successful and quintessentially Australian films such as *Sunday Too Far Away* (1975) and *The Cars That Ate Paris* (1974).

Back then, and even on occasion now, if you wanted to cast aspersions on anything Australian you'd better watch out. As a Melbourne professor Walter Murdoch said back in 1938:

> 'We Australians are too touchy, as a race, I mean. As individuals, we may be above reproach . . . but collectively we are as sensitive as a cat's whiskers . . . Why should we be so infantile as to want everybody to love and admire us? Why should we resent plain speaking?' [7]

This cultural cringe, so-called, is part of a wider snobbery that I touched on in the previous chapter about Aboriginal people. It came about not just because some Australians felt inferior to their opposite numbers in the mother country, it's because of the way we British people look on at the rest of the world. Like it or not, however enlightened we think we are as a race, and however appalled we feel at the behaviour of our predecessors around the world, the British sense of entitlement is very deeply rooted in us. We do like to think we are the centre of the universe, despite our weather and our current chaotic politics, and our self deprecation. (You have to be pretty sure of yourselves to self-deprecate as we Brits do.)

It's evident too in our attitude towards Aboriginal artefacts. The indigenous people have a real fight on their hands when it comes to reclaiming them. They are up against the might of the British establishment.

∞

Mark Twain had his own method for dealing with the cringe. He travelled to Australia with his wife and second daughter in 1895 for a series of lecture tours. Soon after his arrival at Watson's Bay in Sydney Harbour the press appeared in a boat alongside his, and on being asked what he thought about Australia he said, 'I don't know. I'm ready to adopt any that seem handy.'[8]

Twain, according to writer Don Watson, was the 19th century version of a megastar. If the eyes of Australia had been on Anthony Trollope twenty odd years earlier, both eyes and hearts were now focused on the odd-looking man who was regarded as not just the most famous man in America but the funniest. He'd become rich, and then bankrupted by some bad business decisions, so the Australian tour was Twain's way of recouping some of his losses.

According to Watson Twain (whose real name was

Samuel Langhorne Clemens) was loved throughout the country, and '. . . he knew the proprieties and did not trouble his Australian audiences with social criticism or question with any vigour the direction the Australian colonies were taking.' But that doesn't mean he didn't listen and learn, and comment.

Twain also loved Australia. He loved it for its eccentricities and its differences – in its weather, wildlife, its customs and above all, in the people. He described Sydney as 'an English city with American trimmings', where the manners of the city dwellers were more American than British and conversation was vivacious and uninhibited: 'English friendliness with the English shyness and self-consciousness left out.' He remarked on the accent, as expressed in the announcement of a maid in a hotel: 'The tyble is set, and here is the piper; and if lydy is ready I'll tell the wyter to bring up the breakfast.' And he was thrilled by the expression '*My word!*'

He had a good chortle at the idiosyncrasy of the railway gauges which meant passengers had to be turned out of their seats to change trains on reaching the border between New South Wales and Victoria. 'Think of the paralysis of intellect that gave that idea birth,' he exclaimed. 'One or two reasons are given for this curious state of things. One is, that it represents the jealousy existing between the colonies – the two most important colonies of Australia. What the other one is, I have forgotten.'

He told a couple of tall stories that had been told to him, the more famous of which concerned a man named 'Cecil Rhodes' (whose namesake was Prime Minister of South Africa at the time) and a shark, in whose belly 'Rhodes' discovered a ten-day-old copy of the London *Times* telling him of a fourteen percent increase in the price of wool; as a result of which intelligence he was able to borrow £100,000 from a wool broker to buy up the entire wool stock of New South Wales and make their joint fortunes. The story was told deadpan, implying either that Twain was taken in by it or that he had an advanced sense of irony, which the Aussies would have loved him for.

And then of course there were the Aborigines, about whom Twain wrote at length without ever having met one.

Like Trollope, he regarded the Aboriginal people as clever savages: agile, astonishingly skilled at the 'weet-weet' and the boomerang, but too lazy to build themselves houses. Before the arrival of the white man they kept their own numbers down by infanticide, he said; but 'The white man knew ways of reducing a native population eighty per cent in twenty years', through imported disease or other forms of population control. 'The native had never seen anything as fine as that before.'

He then ritted at considerable length about stories he had heard of landowners poisoning Aborigines with cakes laced with arsenic, about which he declared:

> 'The white man's spirit was right, but his method was wrong. . . In many countries we have taken the savage's land from him, and made him our slave, and lashed him every day, and broken his pride, and made death his only friend, and overworked him till he dropped in his tracks; and this we do not care for, because custom has inured us to it; yet a quick death by poison is lovingkindness to it ..'

He quoted a report in a London journal about an attempt by the French to attract free settlers to the penal colony of New Caledonia.

> 'The Governor expropriated the Kanaka cultivators from the best of their plantations, with a derisory compensation . . .' So the

migrating settlers 'found themselves in possession of thousands of coffee, cocoa, banana, and breadfruit trees, the raising of which had cost the wretched native years of toil whilst the latter had a few five-franc pieces to spend in the liquor stores of Noumea.' Twain described this as as 'robbery, humiliation, and slow, slow murder, through poverty and the white man's whisky. The savage's gentle friend, the savage's noble friend, the only magnanimous and unselfish friend the savage has ever had, was not there with the merciful swift release of his poisoned pudding.'

What the Australians made of Twain's thoughts, or the way in which he expressed them, I have no idea.

He wound up with the immortal saying:

'There are many humorous things in the world, among them the white man's notion that he is less savage than the other savages.'

∞

DH Lawrence spent 99 days in Australia, first in WA and then in Sydney, where he wrote the bulk of his book *Kangaroo.* I have only read a few chapters of this, enough to know that the central character Lovat Somers – believed to be closely based on Lawrence himself – was struggling with finding himself living in a country where no one was BETTER than anyone else, only BETTER OFF (his caps). 'In old, cultured, ethical England' the distinction between RESPONSIBLE and IRRESPONSIBLE members of society was clear-cut, but this distinction did not seem to exist in Australia. No one appeared to have authority over anyone else, or if anyone did choose to give orders they would not necessarily be obeyed, which in Lawrence/Somers' mind meant Australia was in danger of running close to

ANARCHY.

It's interesting, as I see it, to witness the confusion of a man brought up in a country with clear class divisions going back centuries, finding himself in a country where notions of class did not exist; and where distinctions between the people depended not so much on background as on how much money they had.

The book is not regarded as one of Lawrence's best apparently, particularly in Australia where he was looked on as 'a day tripper whose knowledge of Australia came from a few months at Thirroul reading the *Bulletin*.'[9] It appears Lawrence had arrived in Australia with high hopes of finding a Utopia, an antidote to the degeneration and corruption of England, and left deeply disillusioned.

One of the better known 'plastic bags' – writers and journalists, for the most part, who fly in to a place, make a lot of noise and fly out again leaving nothing behind[10] – was Bruce Chatwin, the travel writer and archaeologist, who spent a short time in Australia investigating nomadism and Aboriginal song for his book *Songlines*. Once again his book came in for much criticism, partly because it was written as a novel with the author at the heart of it – much like *Kangaroo* – and it was never clear what was fact and what was fiction, and partly because Chatwin relied on white intermediaries in his researches rather than direct contact with Aboriginal people. Not least, he had committed the cardinal sin of not spending enough time in the country he was writing about. (Chatwin was a man in a hurry – at the time he was researching and writing *Songlines* he was already suffering from the illness that eventually killed him at the age of 48.)

Bill Bryson's *Down Under: Travels in a Sunburned Country* was loved by readers and sold zillions of copies but was on the receiving end of considerable stick by some critics, not least because of its popularity. Kathy Lette said in *The Sunday Telegraph*, 'Any decent publisher would have ordered the author to spend another six months with his subject – but hey, this is Bill Bryson.'[11] He was accused of being patronising and egotistic and his book was dismissed as shapeless and thin, with feeble jokes, and offering nothing new or perceptive about the country he hadn't spent enough time in.

Attitudes towards these 'plastic bags' has softened over the years by and large. But an outsider who criticises Australia without having spent several years in the country should still watch out. To quote the correspondent to the *Gympie Times* back in Trollope's time: 'A just criticism of Australian affairs can only be written after much patient philosophical inquiry.'[12]

Message received loud and clear.

Chapter 6

Sydney's beach wars

Think of Australia and you think of beaches. There are thousands of miles of them, mostly spread around the coast, stretching into infinity. White sand, yellow sand, coarse sand, sand so fine it slips through your fingers like silk. Endless ocean-side strands for surfers, cosy coves for the rest of us. And many of them within such easy reach of the city centre you can jump on a bus and go for a lunchtime swim and be back before your workmates notice your absence.

Australian beaches are not like European beaches. It's true they are havens for sunbathers – or 'sun bakers' as they are referred to in Oz, which bearing in mind what the sun does to the skin is probably more apt – but they are also sports training grounds for young things racing up and down the sand and in and out of the sea training to be lifesavers; or intrepid amateur swimmers pounding the waves from Bondi to Bronte, or Cottesloe Beach to Rottnest Island in the west. Most Sydney beaches have rock pools for those of us who don't want to be beaten black and blue by the ocean surf. But even the pools are for serious swimmers mainly, and swimming galas. No Australian *ever* does the breaststroke, which means you can spot a pom a mile off.

Australians are at home on the beach. Unlike the Brits they have not had to save up for a year and fly for several hours in order to enjoy a couple of weeks of sand, sea and sunshine. The beaches and the oceans are part of who they are. So it came as a shock to me to find out this was not how it always was. As I delved into the history of Australian beach culture I uncovered a weird and wonderful soap opera of legislation, lawlessness, fashion mishaps and general outrage.

It began when I started looking into the history of Manly – where my g-g-grandfather lived for a while and where his son, my g-grandfather, was alderman for a number of years. I came upon a story about a bunch of young men who moored their boat off Manly beach after a day's fishing in September 1902, plunged over the side into the water and were promptly arrested and taken to the local police cell.

It appears that sea bathing at that time was prohibited between daylight hours by local by-law courtesy of Manly Council, and policed by someone with the glorious title of Inspector of Nuisances, whose duties also included removing dead animals from the street. Whether or not these particular lads were wearing anything at the time is not on record.

The story then goes that the editor of the local newspaper, a Mr Gocher, announced in print his intention to swim the following day in broad daylight by way of protest, expecting to be arrested. It took him three goes before the police finally took any notice, escorted Mr Gocher to the police station, politely questioned him and then sent him home. But he kept up his protest and a year later, in November 1903, the law was rescinded, and daylight bathing was permitted on condition that everyone over the age of eight wore a costume covering themselves from neck to knee.

This anecdote, which I gleaned from a book called *Manly and Pittwater, its beauty and progress*, written by P W Gledhill and published in 1948, is not the full story of course. Mr Gocher was not the only or even the first person to protest against the ban. There were plenty of others, including individuals such as Arthur Lowe, who claimed he'd been surfing since he was a young lad, riding the waves at 6am on his own as nobody else wanted to desert their beds at that hour, who dismissed Gocher's protest as a publicity stunt and claimed credit should properly go to the group of surfers who held a mass 'surf-in' at Bondi.[1]

I discovered the ban originated with Governor Macquarie, who in 1810 spotted some men cavorting in the water at government wharf and pronounced bathing an 'indecent and improper custom'. The ban was expanded by subsequent governors to include 'all water exposed to public view between 6am and 8pm'.[2] Whether or not the bathers were clothed is not disclosed, but judging by paintings of that time and later, including Tom Roberts' *The Sunny South* (1887), chances are they weren't.

It was a problem not so much of health and safety as of public decency. As the population in the 19th century grew, and changed, and new middle-class migrants from the old country brought new concerns with status and respectability, so 'the anarchic bathing practices hitherto enjoyed by the less respectable classes' was no longer deemed acceptable.[3]

Needless to say the law was often flouted, deliberately or out of ignorance, and many local councils turned a blind eye. Some of the better off residents acquired bathing machines, but the idea never caught on, partly because the wheels got stuck in the sand, and partly because the tiny enclosures they held gave the occupant no opportunity to swim properly.

Despite the ban bathing grew in popularity in the latter part of the 19th century and rock pools sprang up on many ocean beaches, though their use was strictly segregated. Manly council even erected a fence down the middle of the beach to separate the sexes, though since the fence did not extend into the sea itself it was pretty much a waste of time. In March 1902 Sydney women competed in their first major swimming carnival in the presence of male spectators, though for the sake of decorum they were ordered to cover themselves with cloaks immediately before entering and after leaving the water.

In 1894 the New South Wales Legislative Council debated the topic of public bathing at some length, with no conclusion, as members could not agree on what was considered appropriate clothing.[4] (It's worth bearing in mind that 1894 was still the Victorian period, when ladies' legs were firmly covered to and beyond the ankle and were only ever revealed in public in pantomime.)

Then, most glorious of all, came the 'skirt' controversy.

In 1907 the Mayors of Waverley, Bondi and Manly proposed a regulation making it compulsory for both men and women to wear 'skirted' costumes for sea bathing. This not surprisingly produced ridicule and outrage, as expressed by one correspondent to a newspaper, who spluttered:

> 'They go altogether too far. Why should these three Mayors seek to revolutionise civilisation by enforcing a man to wear a woman's costume simply because he is bathing? . . . Bathers are the most manly of men . . . they would not for a minute tolerate the wearing of women's clothes. The manly woman may be possible, but save us from the womanly man.'[5]

(This last comment also tells us something of the

prevailing attitude towards the sexes.)

The following Sunday morning on a crowded Bondi beach a group of men emerged together from the dressing rooms. Among them was a tall skinny lad wearing 'a long, red muslin dress'.

> 'The tall youth proceeded to the water's edge, and, holding up his skirt, allowed a breaking wave to wet his feet. Immediately this event occurred the most weird and blood-curdling cries rent the air, and a small array of skirted life-savers rushed to the scene, and rescued the "maiden" in trouble.'[6]

The men then formed a procession and marched in line from one end of the beach to the other. They were dressed in a mixture of ladies' evening dresses, petticoats and other female undergarments, tablecloths, coloured long skirts, a 'grandmother's wedding dress' with a train born by train-bearers, picture hats and gladiators' costumes.[7] They bore banners bearing a large empty jam tin representing the Mayor's head and a dead bird representing the aldermen.

There were cheers, and chants, and photographs, and general merriment all round. Similar carefully choreographed protests against the 'skirt' were happening at Manly and Coogee at the same time, all designed to make a right mockery of the new regulations.

The bathing skirt, needless to say, died a quick death.

(I did a quick search for photos and found one in the *Sydney Mail*, 23 October 1907, of a large group of men dressed in everything from baby's bonnets to Roman togas and what looks like an Elizabethan jester's costume.)

The Mayor of Waverley, Mr Watkins, subsequently denied having insisted on 'skirts' and claimed he and his fellow mayors had been misunderstood. The Mayor of Manly declared 'Skirts! I know nothing of men having to wear skirts . . . My opinion is that Waverley's Mayor had not grasped the facts of the case.'[8]

So I did a bit more digging and discovered an interview between Watkins and a journalist from the *Evening News* on 12 October. In a conference the previous day with the Mayors of Randwick and Manly, Watkins said the three of them had agreed on a 'patent combination that would preserve decency', which he described like this:

> 'It is a combination consisting of a guernsey with trouser legs, and reaching from near the elbow to the bend of the knee, together with a *skirt* [my italics], not unsightly, but simply attached to the garment, and covering the figure below hips to knee; also covering the outer garment, and attachable or attached.'[9]

They had arranged for David Jones and Co to have a sample made which would be on view at the Waverley Council Chambers for all to see. And yes, he was perfectly happy to wear such a garment. And, finally:

> 'By-the-bye, you might point out that under our new system there can be no duplication of bathing dress. The one pattern, will answer for the women as well as the men. All must be covered in apron or skirt fashion.'

Unequivocal, you could say.

It was a brief episode that lasted less than a month, but it was not only a great story, it's a nice example of the Aussie attitude to the daftest aspects of officialdom.

Up until around the 1940s both men and women were forbidden from exposing their chests, or their backs, and away from the beach they had to wear jumpers or shirts over their costumes. Then after the war along came the bikini – invented by a Frenchman and named after the Atoll (no one seems to know why). There is a photo in the

Sunday Sun newspaper taken in 1945 of two young women on Coogee Beach cavorting in skimpy and frilly two-pieces while a bunch of appreciative young man wearing one-pieces look on.[10] But as late as 1956 a Bondi beach inspector ordered some girls off the beach for wearing the bikini, with the pronouncement: 'I came to the conclusion the scantier the girl's costume the scantier her brains.'[11]

Behind all the puritanism and the legislation it seems lay the idea that the beach and the sea were to be used for their health-giving properties and nothing else. They were not meant to be *enjoyed*. So once ocean bathing was allowed rules still existed about what a person was allowed to do when she or he was not in the water. He/she covered up, in a coat or a dressing gown, and was meant to make her/his way to and from the water as quickly as possible without *loitering* – or as one man put it: 'the promiscuous laying about after a dip.'[12] The Mayor of Randwick decreed that it was all right for a man or woman to stop to talk to a friend on the beach so long as she/he was wearing an overcoat.[13]

The idea of just standing around enjoying the warmth of the sun on one's (covered) back, or heaven save us actually *lying down* on the sand and sunbaking was quite beyond the pale. The Manly authorities eventually caved in enough to provide specially fenced-off areas for sunbathers, but anyone caught enjoying a bit of sun outside these areas could be fined.

Despite the problem with correct clothing beach resorts began appearing on the coasts of all the major towns in the 19th century, beginning with Botany Bay in the 1840s and spreading to Bondi, Balmoral and The Spit, and especially Manly, which was deliberately modelled on Brighton in England and promoted to country people as a place to breathe good sea air. There were piers with aquariums and kiosks, and huge amusement grounds. People picnicked in their Sunday best. It was like little England transported thousands of miles across the oceans, despite the radically different conditions. If the general public were not allowed to swim they would do everything else the English enjoyed in their rather chillier seaside resorts.

Surfing was also becoming popular. It originated with the Aboriginal people – Captain Cook remarked on it back in the 1780s – and was encouraged by the authorities, again for its invigorating and beneficial qualities, and because it was considered to be democratic, since 'duke's son and cook's son can . . . derive enjoyment from it; and its cost is practically negligible.'[14] The enthusiasm for surfing brought an increased danger of death by drowning however. Cue the arrival of another Australian icon: the lifeguard.

When I was in Australia one of my favourite TV programmes was a series called *Bondi Rescue.* It was effectively an extended PR exercise on behalf of the bronzed, honed and beautiful lifesavers on Bondi Beach – exclusively male, oddly enough. All human life was there. Not only did these Adonises rescue swimmers in trouble – invariably tourists swimming the wrong end of the beach and not within the flags (we've all done it, and you only do it once; either you drown or you learn a lesson). They hunted for, and found, lost children, comforted distraught parents, dealt with sufferers of sunstroke or drunkenness or over-imbibing of mysterious substances. My favourite episode featured a bunch of Chinese tourists who arrived by coach direct from the airport and raced off down the beach and into the water before anyone had a chance to yell 'watch out for the jellyfish!' (The balm for which, as I remember, is vinegar. But don't take my word for it.)

The Australian lifeguard is an icon: the bush may have its swagman, squatter and sundowner, but it's the lifeguard who adorns the posters and the postcards, with his rippling muscles, his quaint little cap and his confident grin. He epitomises the Aussie spirit: brave, fit, and ready for anything: 'A gladiator caste, envied by all men, adored by all women.'[15]

But his history – and it appears very much to be 'his' – is apparently quite different. Lifeguards were not always pillars of respectability. As often as not they were larrikins with vandal tendencies, who with a few pints inside them would get up to all sorts of capers such as tearing down fences on beaches at night-time and making bonfires out of them. They invented larky initiation ceremonies such as digging a hole in the sand into which they threw the young recruits and proceeded to urinate and vomit on them. They had a cheerful, and very Aussie, contempt for authority and were often at odds with officialdom.[16]

Men became lifeguards not always for altruistic reasons. (Women were excluded because they were considered too weak.) As often as not they joined the clubs for social advancement, or to have access to the facilities, rather than for the honour of saving lives. At the same time there were many stories of astonishing bravery and selflessness. Nowadays there are professional lifeguards on duty at all the major beaches in the summer months, paid for by the local councils and boosted by volunteers at weekends and bank holidays, and I imagine there's a good deal of kudos attached to the job.

I had my own close encounter with one of them when I lived in Australia in my youth. I was swimming outside the flags (yes, I know, I hadn't been in the country long) and couldn't figure out why no matter how hard I paddled the shoreline seemed to be receding further and further away. I did not then, and don't really now, understand the power of the rip. So I waved and my boyfriend at the time waved back, and then lo and behold a young stranger looking not a day older than fifteen pounded through the surf towards me, yanked me back to the shore, and while I lay panting on the sand like a beached whale he looked down at me with a smirk, winked and said: 'You only did that so you could meet a lifeguard, dincha?'

But the greatest glory of all about the Australian beach and all it has to offer is that it's free. FREE! All right it costs a bit to park, or in bus fares, not to mention the odd dollar or five on juices or iced coffees. But the beach and the ocean and the rock pools – with the odd exception – are open to all for nothing.

But again, it wasn't always like that. Nineteenth century land grants often included bits of shoreline, which made it out of bounds to the general public. In 1906 a commercial operation called Wonderland City erected an eight-foot wire fence at Bondi which blocked access to the beach. So kids just cut the wire. When the company applied for a licence to continue trading protesters lobbied parliament, and stopped them. Privately owned beaches were bought back from their owners. Beaches belonged to the people and woe betide any organisation or individual who tried to appropriate them.

In 1999 the producers of the American TV show *Baywatch* began filming on Avalon Beach, and any member of the public who tried to use the beach or the surf was removed. This brought the following response from a protester in the *Sydney Morning Herald*:

> 'We're used to *Home and Away* but they only use three trucks and mostly use the far end of Palm Beach. *Baywatch* had 15 trucks and, frankly, they had a Hollywood approach, thinking they were God's gift to the beach.'

In return, the producer of *Baywatch* labelled the protesters:

'Very non-Australian. These are people who don't want

to share things, like surfers who don't want to share the wave . . .'[17]

Nice try, Mr Hollywood producer. Of course the opposite is true. Australians own their beaches and no one is going to tell them otherwise.

I was in Sydney in 2000 during the build-up to the Olympics and I heard about plans to build a volleyball stadium smack in the middle of Bondi Beach, which was causing no end of controversy. It was not just the appropriation of the public space people were protesting about, it was the possible lasting damage the building would cause to the beach. So I hastened down there to watch the excitement as they dug the first pegs into the ground, but by the time I arrived all I found was a large fenced-off section with a security guard standing on each corner, and not a protester in sight. The building went ahead despite everything, and the world in general rejoiced to be able to see the magnificent views of the globally-famous and iconic Bondi Beach in the background of the matches. The stadium was removed the moment the Games were over and as far as I am aware the beach survived intact, and life went on.

Chapter 7

Town and country

Tourists to Australia rarely venture far inland, except perhaps to take a look at Uluru (formerly Ayres Rock) and Kata Tjuta (formerly the Olgas). I confess when I lived there in my twenties I stuck pretty firmly to the coast. Why desert those glorious beaches for endless miles of scrub?

It is only scrub to the ignorant of course. Country Australia is, arguably, where the heart of Australia lies. Cities, you could also argue, are much the same throughout the western world, with their chain restaurants, crowded streets and stress. But outback Australia is unique for a number of reasons.

Australia is a big country. It is almost as large as the US, and most of Europe could fit in it snugly. It has a fraction of the population of both those continents – at latest count the US has 325 million and Europe 743 million to Australia's 25 million.[1] [2] [3] So it's no wonder there are parts of inner Australia which appear to be completely uninhabited by human beings.

Apart from my own fleeting trip to Uluru and an overland journey on a guided tour from Alice Springs to Darwin, I have never explored the outback proper. I did once harbour a dream of hiring a four-wheel vehicle and setting off around Australia on dirt tracks. The nearest I got to that was a two-day 500 km drive, with my brother, from Uluru to Alice Springs via Kings Canyon, part of it on the Mereenie Loop, an untarmacked road that had been closed until the day before because of flooding. We drove across rivers in full flood and survived one puncture, after which we continued in total silence as we only had one spare tyre and we were both, it later transpired, terrified that a second puncture would entail not only waiting indefinitely for a passing truck to stop and help us, but a $2000 emergency callout fee. That was as close as I have ever managed to get to playing the fearless pioneer.

Australia's sparse population has entirely to do with water, or the lack of it. Most of the interior of the continent is desert. The average farm has to be several hundred or even thousand times larger than the British equivalent to produce the same amount of foodstuff. Many farmers even now lead lives of unimaginable remoteness.

You'd have to be relatively mad to be a farmer in Australia. No matter how canny you are or how good at business, there's nothing anyone can do about that vicious climate. Droughts seem to be the norm these days. A few years ago I spent some time on a farm in New South Wales during a drought and my farmer friend was having to spend $1000 a day – *a day* – on feed for his sheep. While I was there the police called round to talk to his manager. Apparently the manager's ex boss had had a breakdown and the police were checking to see if the manager might have lent him a gun. That is what many farmers do in extreme circumstances – shoot their stock and reserve the last bullet for themselves.

If the drought doesn't get you the floods will. Or bushfires, which are common occurrences, not just in outback Australia. I was there during Black Saturday in 2009, when the worst fire on record killed 173 people and an estimated one million animals in Victoria. In 2003 a fire destroyed large swathes of park and bushland in the ACT and New South Wales and reached as far as the suburbs of Canberra, killing four people and burning hundreds of houses. It takes very little – a lightning strike, a discarded cigarette, a spark from a barbecue or in one case I witnessed a fire-cracker – to set off an inferno that can destroy thousands of acres in minutes.

Bushfires, droughts, floods and sandstorms aside, there is something magical about countryside Australia. Parts of it are breathtakingly beautiful in a way that is quite foreign to us in the UK, with our neatly-hedged fields and picture-book greenery. If you're a Brit, used to the skyline being less than a mile away, those open roads and distant horizons can blow your mind. Everything is on a massive scale, whether it's landscapes, mountains, roads, shorelines, or cartons of fruit juice you can barely lift. I swear the Aussies have more sky than we have. They certainly have more stars, and they're closer and twenty times brighter. Their birds are bigger and louder than ours. Their weather is more extreme than we can ever imagine – droughts, fires, floods, gales, rain- or sandstorms – you name it, they have it fiercer, more sudden and infinitely more unpredictable.

The eastern Australia country town usually comprises one main street and a population of anything from around 500 to 20,000. On a weekday it may look deserted, and at any time it may seem as if not much goes on there.

These towns were once vital centres where farmers came to buy tools or seeds or dresses, swap gossip and drown a beer or two in the hotel. Nowadays many of them are struggling to survive, so they earn their living wooing passing travellers with what you might call a USP, or Unique Selling Proposition.

My favourite USP-town was a tiny place called Ouyen

in Victoria. It has a population of just over 1,000, and it was known as the Vanilla Slice Capital of Australia. We visited it during the drought of 2003, just after a group of five hundred women, not all of them from Ouyen, had been transported in a convoy of buses to a secret location where they stripped off and did a raindance. (There's a strategically blurred record of it on YouTube.) It didn't work, though as one participant said it did help to take people's minds off the awfulness of the drought.

Then there is Cowra (pop 10,000), in New South Wales, best known for its wonderful Japanese gardens and for the mass breakout of Japanese and Italian prisoners of war back in 1944, when hundreds of Japanese died. In the local tourist centre in a remarkably clever exhibition the hologram of a young girl guides you through the events that led to the largest POW breakout in modern history.

The town of Young (pop 7000), is home of the prune and renowned for its cherries. A few years ago it also hosted 90 or so Afghan asylum seekers who saved the town's abattoirs from closing – thereby contributing $2 million to the economy, according to the mayor – and who became so popular that when their temporary visas expired the locals campaigned for them to stay.

At Hay (pop 2000) we visited what was then a brand new Shearers' Hall of Fame, where you can learn more than you thought you wanted to know about sheep shearing. You can watch shearers at work in a genuine shearing shed, try your hand at shearing a sinister tin sheep that yelps when you 'cut' it, or sniff sheep pee at the press of a button.

Coomealla (pop c800) is etched on my brain forever for its 'parmi upgrade'. I can't remember how we ended up there but the only place to get a meal was at the Coomealla Memorial Club. Australia's clubs are iconic, and unique to Australia. They are mostly kept afloat by the takings from poker (fruit) machines, and they offer more or less edible food in unpretentious surroundings for a pittance. We arrived on 'Schnitzel night' - $7.50 for a plain schnitzel or $9 for a 'parmi upgrade' (schnitzel with parmigiana sauce). The parmi upgrade is now a running joke in the household of my brother and his family.

Holbrook (pop 1,000), in the middle of nowhereish New South Wales, has a 'best-kept secret' otherwise known as a pottery museum. It has a comprehensive display of nearly 2,000 pieces of pottery from early colonial days and is privately owned by a couple of ceramics experts, Geoff and Kerrie Ford, who have written books on the subject. I was the only visitor at the time I was there but for anyone interested in such things it's a must. There is a small entrance fee, and photography – to the disgust of some tourists – is not allowed.

Then there is Tasmania, home to the (extinct) Tasmanian tiger and to inhabitants with two heads.

This is not my joke. How tasteless would that be. It's what the man at the booking office at MONA told us. MONA, the Museum of Old and New Art, is situated just outside Hobart and is entirely underground. Again it's privately owned, by a man named David Walsh, who made his dollars from gambling, and it contains everything from Norman Lindsay and Ai Wei Wei to a number of modern and sometimes blushingly subversive artists and sculptors from all over the world. The website gives you a flavour of the place itself.[4] If you are a local and have two heads – to quote the guy at the desk – you can get in for free.

Also in Tasmania, smack in the middle of nowhere, was The Wall. This again was an ambitious and privately-funded project, conceived by sculptor Greg Duncan. It consisted of a series of three-metre high timber walls, on which Duncan had carved, in relief, the history of the (white) men and women who made Tasmania. It was housed in a modern warehouse when we visited a few years ago, a work in progress, one of the most impressive and original works of art I've ever seen.

At the risk of this turning into a travelogue, Tasmania commemorates its convict past on its western side at Macquarie Harbour, where you can attend 'Australia's longest running play', *The Ship That Never Was*, performed outdoors on the banks of the harbour. It tells in irreverent style the story of a bunch of convicts who escaped from Sarah Island, stole the boat they were building and managed to sail it to Chile, where they lived for two years before being captured. The following day the same actors will take you on a cruise along the Gordon River, stopping off for a guided tour of Sarah Island – now a haven for wildlife and flora, but back then one of the toughest penal stations for the most hardened 19th century convicts. Meanwhile in the south of the Island there are the remains of Port Arthur, a large prison notable for introducing the Jeremy Bentham-inspired idea of solitary confinement for prisoners as a more effective punishment than flogging or hard labour. It is now a World Heritage site, and with the sun shining on it at a certain angle it looks remarkably like Chatsworth House in Derbyshire.

Australia is one of the oldest continents in the world – Sydney itself sits atop several ancient (and defunct) volcanoes – and Aboriginal rock art is the oldest to have been discovered anywhere. And while they often apologise for the short span of their (colonial) past Aussies are hugely proud of local achievements, and local history. They research and preserve and wherever possible they display it. Virtually every country town has a museum and a historical society, and family historians have filled in the gaps. So you could say colonial Australia is the most chronicled country in the world.

Chapter 8

Sydney Opera House

Many years ago I read what I remembered as a rather turgidly written yet enthralling book about the making of Sydney Opera House. It told the story of two men: Jorn Utzon, the Danish architect, and Ove Arup, the British-born Danish Norwegian engineer, an eccentric who ate ice cream with a fork. I remember little other than the bare bones (and the ice cream), except that it was a tale of an extraordinary relationship between two visionaries: the man who dreamed a design that virtually no one in the world considered possible, or practical, or even desirable, and the man who ate ice cream with a fork and made the dream come true.

All I could remember of the book's title was that it covered only part of the long saga that was the building of the Opera House. So imagine my delight when a hunt on Google and then Amazon turned up *Opera House: Act One*, by David Messent, followed by my joy when the book itself plopped onto my doormat less than a week later.

I quickly discovered it could not be the same book, as it contained forensically-researched and -detailed descriptions of not just every moment and inch of the Opera House's design, but lengthy biographies of most of the many hundreds of people who worked on it. I didn't think I would have stuck with such a book all those years ago, and even now I confess I skimmed some of the more technical stuff in my hunt for the remarkable human story at the heart of it.

I could find no mention of Ove Arup eating ice cream with a fork (and I know I didn't make that up). But amid all the politicking and the manoeuvring lay the makings of what would make the most riveting film, or play, or – perhaps most appropriately – opera. The *Sydney Opera House Opera* doesn't quite sing, excuse the pun, but there's no question the story behind the Opera House is the stuff of high drama.

If you believe, as many people do, that the building is unique, and iconic, and places Sydney more firmly on the map in the eyes of the world than no matter how many images of cricket or kangaroos or boomerangs, it's worth bearing in mind its very existence defied all the odds.

In a nutshell, here's what happened:

In the 1940s a British-born Belgian conductor named Eugene Goossens was lured to Sydney with the offer of a handsome salary plus expenses to take charge of the Sydney Symphony Orchestra. In the course of his stay he decided Sydney Town Hall was inadequate as a concert hall, and so he began to campaign for a brand new, purpose-built building which could house concerts, opera and drama, and he chose Bennelong Point as the ideal site.

The premier of New South Wales, Joe Cahill, took up the idea with gusto, despite the fact that no one had ever seen him attend a concert in his life and he was more likely to be found on the race track. Cahill managed to persuade the Department of Transport to move its bus depot – what had until recently been a tram depot – which was currently occupying Bennelong Point, and for the Overseas Terminal to be shifted to the opposite site of

Circular Quay. Then he set up an international competition to find the best design.

The competition attracted 227 entries from all over the world. The judges were four architects: two from Australia, one from the US and one from Britain. They unanimously chose the design of Jorn Utzon, a Danish architect, despite the fact that the design broke many of the competition's rules and had not been verified by an engineer.

The NSW government appointed the company of Ove Arup, which was based in London (and still is), to act as engineers. Cahill then insisted that building begin almost immediately, before the design for the roof had been finalised.

The original estimate for the cost of building – at AU£3.5m (AU$7)[1] – was set ludicrously low, partly because Cahill believed the state government would never give the go-ahead if they knew the true cost. He also wanted it to be well under way, if not finished, while he was still in office.

The building that was supposed to take two years to build actually took fourteen, and the cost was well over ten times the original estimate.

In the course of it Cahill died, and responsibility for the construction went from an Executive Committee to the Department for Public Works. The first major problem arose when the contractors working on phase one, who had themselves under-tendered, threatened to take the government, the architect and the engineers to court for under-payment. The case was settled out of court.

Ove Arup believed Utzon to be the finest architect he had ever worked with, and he was determined to make Utzon's utopian design work, despite the difficulties. The two men enjoyed a warm and mutually respectful relationship for the first three years until their major falling-out, when Utzon accused Arups of trying to take over from him and of conspiring against him behind his back.

After nine years Utzon resigned, partly over the state government's refusal to pay him for work he had carried out some years earlier, and partly because he felt his role as the architect and overall chief of the project had been undermined. A local architect took over from him and the building was completed, with amendments but still retaining Utzon's original concept, ready for its grand opening in 1973. Utzon never saw the finished Opera House, nor did he ever visit Australia again. The rift between him and Ove Arup was never mended.

∞

This story left me thinking that not only do miracles often arise out of chaos, but that it is virtually inevitable. A less visionary, more practically-minded judging panel would have insisted on seeing an engineer's feasibility report on the winning design, or they would have disqualified it for breaking some of the competition rules. A less visionary, more practically-minded engineer would have insisted on modifications to the design from the start. A less ambitious state premier would not have given the go-ahead to such a risky and unpredictable project in the first place, nor had the nous to bend the figures into a more palatable, if transparently unrealistic initial estimate. A more practically-minded Executive Committee would not have signed off on that initial estimate. The whole business only happened because virtually everyone involved in the project behaved, shall we say, bizarrely.

But while I was not able to find any reference to ice cream, it's safe to say the project would never have materialised if it were not for the extraordinary relationship between two mavericks.

Ove Arup was born in England of a Danish father and

78

Norwegian mother and educated in Denmark. He was known as 'a rebel and an outsider' and famed for his integrity. He was chronically absent-minded and often sent his London staff out at lunchtimes to locate his car when he'd forgotten where he'd parked it. [2] It's said he carried a pair of extra-long chopsticks in his jacket pocket for the purpose of pinching food from other people's plates.[3]

He was a philosopher who cared nothing about money and could not understand how anyone could be motivated by it. He could 'talk for hours about almost anything preferably in terms of the abstract rather than the concrete' without ever finishing a sentence; and according to fellow architect Sir Hugh Casson he 'was never one to let facts become the enemy of imagination'. He knew exactly what he was taking on when he agreed to work on the Opera House, despite the lack of finished detail or evidence that such a building was buildable; he was overwhelmingly excited by what he considered to be 'the most marvellous thing that has been built this century' and realised from day one that to compromise on any part of the original design was to ruin the whole thing. 'What we want is to do our utmost to make Utzon's dream come true, at whatever cost to ourselves, as long as we can bear it,' he said.[4] And through thick and thin, he stuck to that intention.

Arup was in his sixties when he took on the project. He suffered from health problems and was often not able to attend crucial meetings and had to send others in his place. But there was one occasion when the New South Wales government called a crisis meeting in Sydney some way into the project which was attended by Utzon, Arup and his assistant Jack Zunz. The premier was looking for assurances that it was actually possible to build an Opera House that would not fall down, so Arup stood up and said he would deal with it. 'And then he rambled. Unfinished sentence followed unfinished sentence.' Trained stenographers struggled to keep up and eventually gave up. However 'if one listened carefully one could get a picture of what he was saying – rather like an impressionist painting. It all made good sense as a whole. He went on for forty minutes, and then just as suddenly as he had started, he stopped . . . Whether the premier and his colleagues understood and agreed to what he said or whether they were fearful that he would start all over again no one will ever know, but he had won the day.'[5]

As for Utzon, he seems to have been much liked, and admired, at least in the beginning, despite his tendency to go absent at crucial times. He had no address or telephone number on his letterhead, and at one point he closed down his Sydney office to go travelling for three months (studying eastern architecture) and was out of touch all that time. He would then turn up out of the blue at the site of the building – 'and lo and behold God appears from Heaven' said Zunz – and complain he had not been kept informed of various goings-on. Arup was remarkably forbearing. He found him inspiring company and the best architect he had ever worked with. 'But he also has some defects . . . Being an aesthete and an aristocrat he is inclined to value inspiring vision more than pedantic truth.'[6]

Considering the continuing tensions, communication between architects, engineers and contractors were on the whole remarkably chipper, at least to begin with. When the contractors announced they were intending to use explosives during the building process Jack Zunz expressed his concerns in verse. But when things began to go wrong between Utzon and Arup they went horribly wrong, and the relationship – on Utzon's side at least – turned positively vitriolic. At one point Utzon bricked up a connecting door between his office and Arup's. Utzon walked off the project after disagreements not just with Arup but with Davis Hughes, the Minister for Public Works – who was notoriously uninterested in anything to do with art or architecture and was described by another architect as 'a philistine and a fraud'[7] – who Utzon declared was not just withholding money due to him but was treating him with contempt.

It was not just the structural complexities and internal squabbling that caused problems. The state government were (understandably) increasingly alarmed at the rising costs and the length of time it was taking to, for instance, get the shape and texture of the tiles right. The project was being run in several different countries – Arups were based in London, Utzon in Denmark and the construction in Australia – and in the days before telex or fax or email or mobile phones; when the only means of communication was a telegram or a dodgy telephone line or snail mail; before the age when computers could do most of the work; when flying from Europe to Australia took two days. And then there was the public reaction to what was increasingly seen as an expensive white elephant. When the state government introduced a lottery to raise funds it was – in my own experience way back when – boycotted by many disbelievers.

But finally, there it was, complete, opened in 1973 by Her Majesty the Queen and housing a huge concert hall, an opera and dance space, three theatres of varying sizes and a recording studio, plus the obligatory cafes, restaurants, 'retail outlets' and bars.

The design was still controversial. Some architects, such as Harry Seidler, considered the building 'poetry, spoken with exquisite economy of words'. Frank Lloyd Wright described it as a circus tent.[8] Frank Gehry said it 'changed the image of an entire country'. Members of the public called it 'the humpback of Bennelong Point'. But it's safe to say most people, Australians and others, think of Sydney Opera House as the jewel in Australia's crown.

Utzon never saw the finished article, nor did he ever set foot on Australian soil again. He was not invited to the opening ceremony in 1973 and his name was not even mentioned in speeches. But in 2003 a kind of reconciliation came about when the Opera House asked him to redesign part of the interior, and named a room after him, which delighted him. His son Jan took over after Utzon died in 2008.

ᛩ

Is there a building, or a major project anywhere in the world, that comes in on time and on budget? That does not grow in unpopularity the more dollars or pounds it consumes and the longer it takes? That once completed is not transformed almost overnight into a national treasure? The mystery is why anyone is surprised.

Utzon was not the only non-Australian architect to fall out with his employers. The American architect Walter Burley Griffin also won an international competition, to build the national capital at Canberra. But he too fell foul of bureaucracy and his plans were either ditched or 'butchered', and he ended up designing incinerators.[9] Frank Gehry's Disney Concert Hall in Los Angeles suffered similar delays, arguments and threats of cancellation. Gehry threatened to walk out when other architects were brought in to complete the job and was only persuaded otherwise when Disney's daughter stepped in with extra cash. The Willy Brandt airport in Germany, due to open in 2020, has been plagued by lawsuits, design problems, rising costs, complaints from local residents and over-estimation as to the amount of money it will make from travelling shoppers.

ᛩ

As a postscript to this story: in October 2018 during the course of an interview with Louise Herron, the Opera House's chief executive, radio 'shock jock' Alan Jones called for her to be sacked for refusing to allow the sails of the building to be used to advertise a horse race. His complaints were upheld by the (Liberal, right-wing) New South Wales premier, who overruled Ms Herron, followed by the (Liberal) Prime Minister Scott Morrison, who described the Opera House as 'the biggest billboard Sydney has.'[10] The shadow (Labor) premier Luke Foley agreed, as did the now current leader of the (Labor) Opposition, Anthony Albanese.

The advertising went ahead despite a public petition against it, and an on-the-spot protest during which torches were shone onto the Opera House in an attempt to interfere with the projection.

You can almost hear Utzon and Arup turning in their graves.

Chapter 9

The National Theatre

The hazards of research being what they are, once again I find myself wandering down an unrelated avenue that has nothing to do with Australia. (You are welcome to skip this chapter.)

Having delved into the origins of the Opera House I began wondering about our own iconic temple of culture here in London, the National Theatre.

The NT cannot and does not pretend to compete with the Opera House aesthetically. It is a windowless concrete 'brutalist' building that dominates the south bank of the river Thames by Waterloo Bridge. Some people admire the architecture; some, like Prince Charles, have likened it to a nuclear power station.

It was designed by British architect Denys Lasdun, who was chosen as a result of a 'competitive interview' as opposed to a competition. (A competition, according to the artistic director of the NT and actor Laurence Olivier, had the disadvantage of 'having to do exactly as you're told by the winner.'[1]) The board, which comprised directors Peter Hall and Peter Brook and designer Tanya Moseiwitsch in addition to Olivier, specifically did not want anyone who had designed a theatre before. 'We wanted to find a new soul', said Olivier.

Denys Lasdun was the only person who walked into the interview room with neither a team of assistants nor an idea. According to Olivier, 'he just sat there . . . that was immensely effective and of course, as he knew perfectly well, quite touching . . . He said surely the most important aspect of what we are talking about is the spiritual one. Oh, my dear! We all fell for that!'

'"Gentlemen," said Lasdun, "I think that my background and my record is sufficient for you to know not only who I am but the way I approach any commission I have, so I have nothing further to say to you." It was breathtaking.'

Lasdun was a Modernist, a disciple of Le Corbusier – as was Utzon – and needless to say at that time he was at the top of his profession. On 22 November 1963, the day President Kennedy was assassinated, he was appointed architect of the new National Theatre.

Lasdun envisaged the exterior as part of the 'urban landscape' of the South Bank, to merge with the concrete of Waterloo Bridge and the recently-built Royal Festival Hall. He was quoted as saying 'I don't want anything to come between people experiencing the theatre and your drama. They have in a way to use the concrete reality of the building, not tarted up in any way. It must just be space, walls, light. And the ornaments of the building are people moving around.'[2]

Architectural 'ornament' was considered a crime in the 1960s, raw concrete 'the heroic and unadorned material of a new, more honest world.' So the NT was conceived as an antidote to the glitzy, elitist, cherub-encrusted West End theatres with their plush velvet curtains and cramped seating. It was a serious structure with serious intentions, built to house Ibsen and Chekov rather than William Douglas-Home and Warren Chetham-Strode.

The idea of a National Theatre had been around since the beginning of the century, and by the time the Queen laid the foundation stone on the South Bank in 1963 it had gone through five different sites and four different architects. It was originally accommodated in the Old Vic Theatre near Waterloo, while the purpose-built building was being constructed nearby on the site of derelict warehouses on the banks of the Thames, which was described then as a polluted, smelly swamp and 'an eyesore on the edge of polite London.'

It's hard to believe now but the south bank of the river had been much of a no-go area until the Festival of Britain began its regeneration in 1952. In Shakespeare's time Southwark – which now houses the new Globe theatre amidst brand new and swanky apartments owned by City financiers – was the place for low entertainment such as bear-baiting, cock-fighting and theatre. And that's how it remained until the 1960s (except for the bear baiting and cock-fighting; and the theatre). There was Bankside Power Station – now Tate Modern – belching out smoke, empty warehouses and deserted docks. No one went there except to catch a train from Waterloo Station.

So did the construction go smoothly? Was it on budget and did it open on time?

I can't pretend it makes as good a story as the soap opera of the Opera House, but the creation of arguably the most successful, prolific and exciting theatre in the world had its fair share of trial and tribulation.

The original brief had been for a 1000-seat auditorium and a 400-seat experimental space, but arguments among the board – creative people all – arose over their format. Olivier fancied the proscenium arch as he claimed he could not do comedy without it and it was the only design suited to comic 'asides' to the audience. Lasdun worked from the inside out, which meant focusing on the relationship between actor and audience. Actors and architects were dispatched to the West End to recite from the stage and gauge at which point 'the magic died', which was deemed to be 675 feet from 'the point of command'.

But what was 'the point of command?'

Tempers flared. Rows and disagreements broke out between 'brilliantly creative theatrical minds – and egos'. Lasdun declared he could not get to the poetic until he had come to grips with the functional, and he could not get to the functional until he had 'an agreed brief'. He was accused of inflexibility, so the creative minds and egos plotted to meet up without his 'intimidating' presence. The NT's Literary Manager (and critic) Kenneth Tynan pompously announced: 'We are paying a man to decorate our house, and if he succumbs to the illusion the house belongs to him, then we must – however regretfully – escort him to the door and engage someone else.'

Lasdun was as confused as anyone. He had always bent over backwards to meet the needs of clients, he just needed those clients to agree what those needs were. His design for the bigger space started out as a square room with a triangular performing space in one corner. This may have been inspired by a picture he had on his office wall of St Mark's Square in Venice – not for the architecture but for the semi-circle of people spontaneously gathered together to watch a street performance. The triangle was eventually softened to become a semi-circle and eventually, after eighteen months, it morphed into an amphitheatre modelled on the ancient Greek theatre at Epidaurus. It was named, appropriately in one sense even though it had no pros arch, the Olivier.

By contrast the Lyttelton, also known as the 'Any other business theatre' – which does have a pros arch – was decided in a week. It was extended at the insistence of the arts minister Jennie Lee, for financial reasons, and ended up with almost as many seats as the cavernous Olivier. The experimental theatre, the Cottesloe, started out as workshops until Peter Hall brought it to life, and under the guardianship of Ian Macintosh of Theatre Projects it was created as a flexible space based on Elizabethan courtyard inns, with a focus on the intimacy between actor and audience.

Who chose these names, and why, is not on record as far as I can see. The Lyttelton and the Cottesloe were named after aristocrats and chairmen of the board. When the Cottesloe was closed for refurbishment it changed its name to the Dorfman in honour of Lloyd Dorfman, founder and ex CEO of the currency exchange company Travelex, who have donated countless fortunes to the National. (Ironically most people I speak to assume it was named after the playwright Ariel Dorfman.) Modern critics such as Michael Billington of the *Guardian* have criticised the decision to name theatres after businessmen rather than writers or actors, partly on the grounds that it creates a precedent and honours commercial enterprise rather than creativity.[3] But that's in the nature of the relationship between art and commerce: the one cannot do without the other.

There is neither the space nor the necessity to go into the slings and arrows of misfortune that beset the actual construction of the National: strikes, the three-day week,[4] rising costs and 25% inflation which – like the under-quoting builders on the Opera House – hit the sub-contractors who'd quoted a fixed price at the start. Much of the stage equipment was state-of-the-art never-been-tried before. And then there was the drum revolve.

They built it in a field. It was – is – five storeys high, sits underneath the Olivier stage and is constructed to operate in two halves independently, so one half of its circular design can carry part of a set up to stage level while the other removes what's there to down below. The problem was they couldn't get it to work. The weight of it crushed the machinery it stood on. It was not until the 1990s that it was fully operational. But when you see what it can do on that vast, open stage, it is nothing short of miraculous.

The building still invites criticism. John Betjeman said it had a feeling of finish and inevitability, like all great buildings. Upmarket journalists called it a masterpiece, 'basically serious, not to say puritanical.' The actor John Gielgud said it was like working in an airport. The tabloid press generally disliked it. And there is no getting away from the fact that it doesn't weather well. When it rains the concrete stains, and the building and its staircases and dark corners under overhangs remind some people of rundown housing estates.

But never mind all that. The National Theatre may not win any beauty contests – and it was Lasdun's misfortune that by the time it was completed in 1976 its brutalist style was already considered out of date – but what may not be considered miraculous outside certainly is inside. Not only does the building produce plays in repertory in all three theatres all the year round, it boasts several cafes, restaurants and bars, on all levels, inside and out, and a 'factory' at the rear of the building where sets, costumes and props are constructed, all on site.

It is also handsomely funded by the British government through the Arts Council, box office takings, income from commercial enterprises such as NT Live and world tours of successful shows such as *War Horse* and *The Curious Incident of the Dog in the Night-Time,* and of course from generous donations from companies such as Travelex

But perhaps most importantly, from Lasdun's point of view, the building is a hive of social activity, open all day to everyone, six and sometimes seven days a week. The terraces outside, fronting the much cleaned-up river – we even have *seals* there now! – are packed to the gunnels all year round, with street entertainment and pop-up booths selling food and drink as far as the eye can see. Thus the architect's vision of a 'democratic' space, plainly designed but functional, open to everyone and where the public are the only ornaments, has been thoroughly fulfilled.

Lasdun was knighted as a result of his efforts, though he never went on to produce any other buildings of particular note. Utzon was awarded the Pritzker Prize, otherwise known as the Nobel prize for architecture. He was part-reconciled with his old enemy the Sydney Opera House, especially when it was declared a World Heritage Site.

Whether either architect ultimately celebrated or regretted their involvement in the creation of these two iconic buildings is another matter.

Chapter 10

The Secret River

Kate Grenville's Booker Prize-nominated book is the story of a Thames boatman, William Thornhill, who is transported to New South Wales in the early 19th century for stealing timber. His wife and two sons travel with him, and after receiving his Absolute Pardon William takes possession of what appears to be a patch of unoccupied land on the Hawkesbury River and imports his family onto it, with mixed consequences.

I admit that unlike most other people I had reservations about the book. I admired it, and Ms Grenville, for the extraordinary breadth of her research, and for her ability to get inside the head of a transported convict. But there was something about the telling of the story I found distancing.

However the stage adaptation blew my breath clean away.

I saw it twice: once in a quarry outside Adelaide back in 2017, and recently at the Olivier Theatre at the aforementioned National Theatre here in London. Nothing beats a quarry in the middle of the bush on a balmy, cloudless night in South Australia in March, but the Olivier Theatre, with its open stage and amphitheatre auditorium, came as close as it is probably possible indoors.

I wrote reviewed both shows on my website, but the more I think about the show, adapted by Andrew Bovell and directed by Neil Armfield, both household names in Australia, the more I see in it.

The big difference between the book and the show is the Aboriginal participation. As Kate Grenville has said, more than once (see chapter 3), she deliberately avoided featuring Aboriginal people as central characters in her book as she did not feel entitled to speak on their behalf. Armfield and Bovell managed to solve that conundrum with the help of a man of Aboriginal origin called Richard Green, who speaks Dharug, the local language of the Hawkesbury. With his involvement and with the aid of the cast, through workshops, Aboriginal people are at the heart of the stage show, speaking untranslated Dharug. This means sections of the play are incomprehensible to English-speakers, which has caused some controversy; but it means we get to see things from the point of view of the convict William Thornhill, and we experience his confusion and, most importantly, his fear.

What is so special about this show – quite apart from its setting, the music, the birdsong, the staging and the acting – is the even-handed way in which Grenville, and Bovell, present their characters. In these post-colonial-guiltily sensitive times it is easy to see the indigenous Australians as the goodies and the colonists as baddies. *Secret River*, without making excuses for what the Brits did back then, shows us how much more complicated the story was.

Thornhill is a convict, unlike my ancestors, who were settlers. My folk were granted 200 acres of land upriver of Thornhill, at a similar time, on a patch of land set back from the frequently-flooding Hawkesbury River. Both families were there out of necessity, though of different kinds. My family were down on their uppers back in their home in Dorset. Thornhill – a fictional character but based closely on Grenville's ancestor Solomon Wiseman – was a convict transported for stealing. The land he acquired on the Hawkesbury was not granted to him. He found it, took it to be 'unoccupied', claimed it, and set up home on it with his family.

My family, Mary Pitt and her five children, may not have had much money – there was no such thing anyway in early colonial New South Wales – but they had status, and connections in the highest places. (See chapter 4.) Thornhill had no status and no connections. Despite his Absolute Pardon all he had to rely on was his skill as a boatman, and his enterprise, of which he had plenty. All he wanted was a piece of land to call his own – something that would have been an impossibility for a man like him back in the old country – to cultivate, build on and ultimately pass on to his children. To 'own' 100 acres of land was an unimaginable dream, but there it was, apparently going begging.

In many ways Thornhill and the Aboriginal people had a lot in common. Both had been displaced from their home and their country. There is a glorious moment in the play when Thornhill and the Aboriginal Elder, Yalamundi, are trying to tell each other in their respective languages and in a good-natured manner to get off their land, which ends in Thornhill declaring – 'Well at least we understand one another.'

Thornhill's younger son quickly makes friends with the Aboriginal children and plays freely and naturally with them. He even wears their clothes – which is to say nothing at all. (In reality the children wear flesh-coloured shorts.) The thumpingly obvious notion that children have no understanding or knowledge of difference, and are

93

quite happy to play with strangers of a different skin colour and language, is woven into the narrative so seamlessly it does not look as if it is Making a Point. But when Thornhill, who is not a bad man by any means and who only has concerns for the survival of himself and his family, beats the child for cavorting with the Aboriginal people (offstage, thank goodness) our hearts are breaking along with the small boy's.

Thornhill does bad things – beating his child is one, killing the indigenous people is another – but out of fear rather than hatred. Other characters in the play are not so sympathetic. Smasher Sullivan treats the Aboriginal people like savages. Thomas Blackwood lives peacefully among them and has set up home with an Aboriginal woman. The whites are all convicts, and while they represent different aspects and attitudes of the interlopers towards the indigenous, there is never a feeling in the play of 'tokenism'. The play ends with Thornhill building a protective fence around his purloined property – the ultimate symbol of western possession.

Like the best plays, or books, *The Secret River* by focusing on one family in one part of Australia at one time manages to tell a much wider story about the colonisation of Australia. Most of the settlers, and many of the pardoned convicts, who travelled to Australia in the early days of its occupation had an ambition to own land – something virtually none of them were able to do in their own country. They were not 'stealing' it, in their view, because – in their view – the original occupants did not appear to own it in the first place. This is the kernel of the tragedy that was colonial Australia. Some of those settlers and convicts were villains and treated the indigenous people shoddily, even violently. Some of them were more enlightened, and did their best to understand them and the differences in their culture. Almost all of them, however humane and far-seeing, assumed they were superior. For a convict who has suffered extreme hardship, both back in his native country and in the new, to be able to consider himself better than someone else was, in the context of the 19th century if not the 21st, understandable.

The play also brought home to me the astonishing opportunities Australia offered to the invading whites back in the early days of colonisation. Free from the centuries-old class system of the old country, where a person's life was more or less defined according to her or his birth, the new colony offered a completely fresh start, where anyone – convict or settler – could be anyone, so long as he or she could lay hands on a piece of land. It was this very freedom, this breakdown of the old system, this equality, that D H Lawrence found so unsettling.

I was particularly interested to see how closely the British public engaged with *The Secret River*. Granted only a few thousand Londoners will have got to see it, but their reaction, both at the time and on social media subsequently, shows there's a better understanding and curiosity here about our colonial Australian past than I'd have given credit for. The pre-play talk with director Neil Armfield and adaptor Andrew Bovell, held in a smallish room rather than in the theatre itself, was sold out the moment it was announced (we managed to sneak in). As Andrew Bovell pointed out – this is your story, here in the UK, the white people depicted in the play were British, not Australian.

To quote one critic in *The New European:* 'An important play: it's time we come to terms with who we really are.'[1]

Chapter 11

Writing the book

Sooner or later it's time to down research tools and start writing the book.

When is research over? Well, never. There's always more to know. And research does not have to be over before you start writing. Inevitably there will be gaps that need filling as you go along, but unless you are on a deadline – in other words a publisher is waiting for your polished work – it is tempting to put this off indefinitely.

In my case I had several false starts, for various reasons. Firstly, I'd never written a period non fiction book before, I didn't know who my readers were, and I could not find the right 'voice'.

Voice is one of those hard-to-define but crucial elements of any piece of writing. You could call it tone, or style, or even intent. It's unique to you, and it will change depending on what genre you are writing in, but the one thing it should be is – much as I hate to use the word – authentic. In other words it must come naturally to you, rather than a style you adopt or copy from someone else. Above all, it should be a pleasure to read.

I have often said, and will say again: anyone can do research. All it takes is time, patience, application and tenacity. The challenge is to turn that research into something that's readable. You will probably remember from your school or college days those impenetrable text books you were forced to wade through in order to get to grips with the Peloponnesian Wars or the Corn Laws. History made dull and incomprehensible and written by people who like to use ten words where two will do, preferably with as many syllables as possible, in the belief presumably that the more obscure the writing the more erudite it is.

That is exactly what I started out doing. In order to prove I had done A Huge Amount of Research and was now an Expert on Early Colonial Australia I made the beginner's mistakes of Putting it All Down and presenting it in what I thought was an Authoritative Manner. But when I read over those early chapters I had to admit, with some dismay, that they read like a series of lectures written, or over-written, by a Pompous Fool who was more concerned about showing off her knowledge than actively engaging with the reader.

So I forced myself to sit back and consider, firstly: who was my reader? I knew from the start that I wanted to appeal to a readership beyond my immediate family, and even at a pinch to people with no particular interest in Australia, or in family history. So I decided to put myself into the book and present my findings not from a strictly objective point of view, like a historian, but as I saw them.

I decided to do something else. In all family history there are gaps. However many facts you can unearth about your antecedents there are bound to be bits missing. Even if you know the what, the where, the how and the when, chances are you don't know the why. In my case, for example, I knew when and how my ancestress migrated to New South Wales, the ship she sailed on and from and to where it sailed. What I did not know was the

Why. Why did a widow of fifty-three, with five children aged from 27 to 14, choose to migrate from Dorset to what was then a penal colony the far side of the world?

So I invented an imaginary scene where my ancestress' cousin paid her a visit and presented her with his proposition that she and her family migrate to New South Wales. I wrote another fictional scene where Mary discussed the proposition with her offspring and they responded in very different ways. I created characters for those offspring in order to generate an argument about the pros and cons of the proposition. I made one daughter a firebrand who somehow knew a good deal about the colony, which she was able to impart to her siblings and thereby to the reader, who argued first against the idea of emigrating and then for it; the youngest daughter who was terrified of leaving her home; another daughter, bored by her dull life and its lack of prospects, who thought it might at least be a distraction; the eldest daughter who tried to moderate between them; and the only son, whose job it was to make the final decision and then to make it all work. In this way I was able to both introduce my characters and tell the story, through them, of what life was like for a struggling rural family at the turn of 19th century Britain, and why that family would consider emigrating across the world to a new colony peopled mostly by convicts.

Those invented scenes of course entailed dialogue. I've been a scriptwriter in my time, and before that an actor, so I have usually found dialogue the easiest part of the equation. But period dialogue is different. We can steep ourselves in Jane Austen or Charles Dickens in order to get a flavour of the way people spoke in those times, but if we wrote exactly as they did we would sound ridiculous.

Modern-day adaptors of period pieces are taking more and more liberties with the language and they are not afraid of the odd anachronism. I don't suppose for a moment Shakespeare actually said, 'God, I'm good!' as Tom Stoppard has him do in the film *Shakespeare in Love.* But it gets a laugh, and it sounds better than, say, 'I am a genius, forsooth!' Today's television audiences are used to hearing modern music behind a period drama, and accents that are closer to Estuary than Eaton Square. The best adaptors are able to play fast and loose with the dialogue while retaining a strong sense of the period.

The 2018 adaptation of Thackeray's *Vanity Fair* is a good example. Becky Sharpe is a 19th century independent and ruthless woman brought right into the 21st century thanks to a bold adaptation by Gwyneth Hughes. I would venture, never having met Ms Hughes, that her first priority was to tell the story and her second priority was to make it meaningful to a modern audience without compromising the reality of mid 19th century Britain. However it seems she found herself having to defend her decision to include a scene where a man argues with his wife against the unthinkable prospect of their son marrying a non-white woman, in the presence of a black servant.

It is tempting to us to look back at history with scorn for the primitive societal values and attitudes to women, or race, or what they would call the underclass. There have even, Lord save us, been moves to censor old texts to make them more palatable to modern sensibility. The best writers from Shakespeare down have been accused of both racism and sexism.

To censor the attitudes of the past is to alter history. No doubt future people will look back at us with astonishment and dismay at the way we treat animals, or the planet, or something we could not begin to conceive of.

But I'm getting on my high horse. Let's just say it is a

delicate business, the juxtaposition of the ancient with the modern. If we judged the heroes of the past by our present-day standards men of the calibre of Mark Twain and Anthony Trollope and countless others would be exiled to Siberia for ten years' hard labour for their attitudes towards race.

So bearing all these rants in mind, it took me a long time to get it right, or as right as I could make it. I sent the first draft to several people for their opinion. One said there was too much of me in it. Another said there wasn't enough. More than one person said I was mixing my genres and should turn the book into a novel. So I went back to the beginning. I kept the invented scenes with my family members but now I peppered the narrative not just with my own observations but with my own experiences of Australia throughout the years. I edited the quotes vigorously. It's far too easy to fill the page with direct quotes, first because it demonstrates authenticity and second because it saves you having to translate what people said into your own words. But too many quotes doesn't make for easy reading and besides, it's lazy. It isn't just what people said that matters, it's how you – and other people – interpreted what they said.

After around six years I had what I considered to be a reviewable draft. I sent it to my editor and she came back with some very useful suggestions, among which was the comment – in response to my query about the specific nature of some of the text which really only had to do with my family – that the more close detail about my family's story the better. That made sense. Detail is colour. She also questioned my use of the word 'native' to mean, well, native. Or more specifically, Aboriginal native. It was a commonly-used word in those days and it was not necessarily used pejoratively. (And as often as not, confusingly, it referred to white people born in Australia.)

But it is not permissible nowadays.

So the book ended up a hybrid: part history, part family history, part memoir and part fiction. A publisher's nightmare, in other words.

And that publisher, on this occasion, was me.

Chapter 12

Publication!

When is a book ready to be published?

In my case, it's when I can't stand the sight of it any more, when I've been through it so many times I hate every word.

I publish my books myself. Independent publishing means the writer has to do everything. The writing is just part of the process, and at times feels like a minor part of it. Apart from hiring a professional editor and cover designer the rest was down to me. Overnight – or over a period of months – I became a publishing house. I learned how to convert a manuscript into the right format for ebooks, design the interior of a paperback, with an index, price it and arrange distribution – which involved setting up my own publishing company – and finally and most crucially, persuade people to buy it. It was a steep learning curve off which I repeatedly tumbled.

But finally there it was. On 15 June 2012, otherwise known as Bloomsday (from James Joyce's *Ulysses*), my first book was officially published.

I threw a party. I created a quiz with an Anglo-Australian theme and divided my guests into teams and awarded prizes. Everyone bought the book. (It was difficult not to.)

I emailed family history magazines and genealogy sites asking for reviews. Some responded, albeit grudgingly, so I fired off several copies of the book to anyone who showed the slightest interest.

The first bookshop I visited with book in hand fell upon it and asked for several copies, which they actually managed to sell. It so happened the lady behind the counter was Australian. This is easy, I thought.

No other bookshop, either in London or Sydney, would even look at the book.

Then I waited.

The first review came from an erudite friend in Australia. He praised the book. Others did likewise, but they were friends. The first significant breakthrough came from the deputy editor of *Family Tree* magazine, who gave it glowing review, as did the Dorset Records Office.

I was astonished. I won't pretend otherwise but I was not really sure the book was all that good. It wasn't just that I knew it so well I hated every word. I had, by mixing the genres, broken a lot of rules. And the book world is full of rules. The remarks were exceptionally pleasing and didn't only talk about the amount of research I'd done. 'Readable', 'page-turning', 'taught me more about my own country than I ever realised.' The best comment I ever received was along the lines of, 'I felt as if she was talking directly to me.'

Hoorah. Job done.

The reception for the first book was positive enough to encourage me to write a second. I went through the usual 'I couldn't possibly write about my great great grandfather who spent all his time on the land, I know nothing about agriculture or the ultra-blokey world of rural Australia', but I did it anyway.

I acquired a small grant from the Royal Australian Historical Society to travel to Moree, in the outer regions of northern New South Wales, to investigate my g-g-grandfather's taking up of land in the region. I made several more trips to Australia and spent several more weeks in libraries studying 19th century Australia. I became engrossed in outback yarns about the bizarre lives and habits of stockmen and sundowners, and I learned enough about droving to go on Mastermind. I steeped myself in Mary Gilmore's colourful memoirs of domestic life in country New South Wales in the late 1800s, and I even came to grips with the origins of Australian politics and inter-colonial disputes in the days before Federation. I kept an eye out for the weird and wonderful such as the multiple railway gauges, I read everything I could find by Henry Lawson and Banjo Paterson and laughed myself off my chair over Paterson's musings on the suicidal tendencies of Merino sheep. I talked to farmers and visited a cattle saleyard. I moved in a world that could not be more different or more distant from my own. I'd like to say I became immersed, but it takes a long time to do that, and I could never spend more than a few months in Australia at any one time. And I was always aware, and I become more so as time goes on, of how very different it is over there.

Friends and acquaintances organised book launches in Australia for my second book, *A Country To Be Reckoned With*. They had no idea what this meant to me. The business of writing is a lonely one and, to repeat what I said in the Introduction, it's hard not to be constantly aware throughout the time it takes to produce a book that no one in the world other than yourself gives a flying saucer what you are writing, or why. To then find yourself standing in front of a roomful of strangers who have travelled especially to see you talk about your book is nothing short of overwhelming.

Writing is hard work. Many people seem to want to be

104

writers, for some inexplicable reason. Many people have started writing a book but never finished it. To have finished and published, in my case, so far six books, three about Australia, is no mean feat – though I say it myself.

But what is most important in my case is how much I have learned about one of the most under-appreciated and overlooked countries in the world. If I feel I have only scratched the surface that is not surprising for someone who doesn't live there. The research and the writing processes, despite the odd drawback, have been some of the most pleasurable occupations of my adult life. In addition, I like to think and hope I have contributed something to the knowledge of that far-off country, my second home, that I love so much and am only now beginning to understand.

Postscript

Australia's bushfires

For several months in late 2019/early 2020 Australia really did become the worst country in the world[1]. Between October 2019 and up until February 2020, as I write this, raging bushfires have destroyed over 11 million hectares of land[2] (27 million acres, almost the size of England), over 2,500 homes, around 33 people including a number of firefighters, and an estimated one billion animals. It was believed some wildlife species were wiped out altogether. Even people not living near the fire regions were affected by smoke, which at one point reached New Zealand and even travelled as far as South America.

It began early, in some cases in September, which is technically spring in the southern hemisphere. I asked a friend, Michael Burge, who lives in northern New South Wales and in the region of a local fire, to tell me his story.

> 'In very early September [2019] bushfires raged through Tenterfield and Drake, destroying homes and other property. Landowners, politicians and the media started throwing around the word 'unprecedented', mainly due to the speed and intensity of these unseasonal fires.

. . . In November 2019 - still spring - fire ravaged two towns in our region (Wytaliba and Torrington) driven by the most intense air movement I have ever experienced. At one point during the terrible day when people were killed at Wytaliba, it felt like we were in the grip of two cyclones fighting for supremacy. The wind was so strong it was shooting into the ground and whipping up slices of soil that shot into the air. Dust, debris and burning foliage were being carried from where the fires were burning at Torrington, 28 kilometres away.

Across the region, we heard of fires travelling ahead of themselves in the form of embers, anywhere between 12 and 40 kilometres ahead of fire fronts during the high winds.

According to climatologists, the hot air ahead of a fire can create a weather system known as a pyrocumulonimbus thunderstorm. I witnessed three of these. One showed on the horizon the day Tenterfield burned, its terrible lava-orange core showing deep within a great cauliflower head. Another was blowing towards our home the afternoon the RFS [Rural Fire Service] messaged me and advised that I leave home or shelter in place, so all I could see of it was the eerie yellow glow that wrapped everything in its pathway.

As I enacted our fire plan and evacuated to Glen Innes, I saw the worst pyrocumulo-nimbus over Wytaliba. It looked like a mushroom cloud after an atomic bomb, although it was collapsing into itself, whipped up by the terrible wind. Collapsing over communities, livestock and wildlife; rivers, creeks and forests. Collapsing over everything I have ever known about living in rural Australia at a thousand metres above sea level in a cool-climate region.'

Wytaliba is a tiny community of around 100 people, living off the grid and away from the public eye, with a school attended by ten children. In thirty minutes on a Friday in November 2019 the whole place went up in flames, obliterating 25 (mostly uninsured) homes, the school, a bridge on the route in, cars, agricultural machinery, wildlife and two local residents.[3] Journalists descended *en masse*, to the dismay of the surviving residents, who'd gone to live there specifically to avoid the maddening crowds. One of them described Wytaliba as 'one big, dysfunctional family', where there were no property boundaries, no mobile coverage, and everyone shared everything.[4]

Within weeks Wytaliba had set up a Facebook page, which I followed, where people were offering to donate everything from toys to clothes to caravans, cars and quad bikes and free holidays for children. They also offered differing views on the causes of the fires, the attitudes of governments – federal and state – the relative uselessness of most insurance companies and questions about compensation and whatever was happening to all those millions of dollars people around the world had donated. One lady piled the burnt and meagre remains of her house onto a truck and deposited them outside Government House in Canberra in protest at their policy – or lack of – on climate change. Fundraising events and morale-boosting community get-togethers sprang up all over the place.

Most residents of rural Australia have a fire plan, or

should have. Here is Michael's:

'Our fire plan is simple. On the evening news every day the fire authorities issue a fire level warning for the following day (this has been in place since the Black Saturday fires in Victoria 2009). If the forecast is Catastrophic (the highest level) then the authorities cannot guarantee the survival of any building or structure, and we have agreed between us that we'll leave early the following morning and get out of the area altogether. If it's Severe or Extreme, we agree we'll stay and keep a close watch on things.

We are not equipped to defend this property as we don't have enough water pressure or a transportable water tank with a generator to hose water onto spot fires or walls of flame. It would be foolhardy to stay without being much better prepared. So, when we leave our property we prepare it by ensuring all doors and windows are closed, the power is off and any fuel or gas tanks (such as the barbecue) are stored away from the house. We have one bag pre-packed with documents, photographs and other irreplaceable mementos, and one bag pre-packed with water, dog food, spare clothing and protective blankets in case we encounter fire when we're on the road. So when we leave it's a matter of dogs and bags in the car, and we just go. We could leave in minutes if required. We have a second way out of our property by car if we get cut off by fallen trees along our main drive.'

Some regional towns are better prepared than others,

and open up community centres or sports grounds to act as temporary evacuations centres.

> 'Despite the support of service clubs and charities on the ground, there was a sense that communities were running out of steam pretty quickly due to the scale of the fires and the length of time critical support was required. Richard [Michael's husband] cooked for the fire services on a few days and described the conditions as very under-staffed and disorganised. In many communities, volunteer fire fighters got no support and were left to find their own meals and drinking water, which has been a big eye opener during this fire season. The state of unpreparedness under the Morrison Government (federal) and the Berejiklian government (NSW state) has been shameful. It's been a combination of "resourcing issues" (according to NSW Rural Fire Service Commissioner Shane Fitzsimmons) and, in Morrison's case, just not listening to the experts who predicted this crisis months, years and decades ago.'

When the fires were almost at their worst, in December, Prime Minister Scott Morrison quietly went on holiday to Hawaii, and it took him a while to decide to return to his burning country and pay the odd visit to affected areas, where he received what might be called a cool reception. Bushfire sufferers and firefighters refused to shake his hand, locals told him in direct Australian terms where he could go.

It wasn't long since Morrison had imported a lump of coal into Parliament and waved it in the faces of fellow parliamentarians and told them not to be afraid of it. Coal rules Australia. 40% of their energy is coal-fired and 7%

comes from renewables.[5] In the UK 9% of our energy comes from coal and 24.5% from renewables[6]. (Not that we have anything to boast about, with a Prime Minister who has confessed he doesn't 'get' climate change.[7]) By contrast Iceland is almost 100% renewable and Costa Rica, Norway and Sweden are not far behind.[8] I even in the course of my climate change meanderings came upon an Australian website whose sole purpose seems to be to put a stop to wind power and other renewables because they're bumping up domestic utility bills.

The right-wing Liberal government are climate change deniers for commercial, economic reasons. Of course. Malcolm Turnbull, Morrison's predecessor, was years ago beaten to the leadership of the Liberal party (by one vote) precisely because of his views on global warming. In 2018 he was ousted from his position as PM for the same reason and replaced by a hard right government of climate change deniers. Denial appears to be deeply endemic in the ruling Liberal party, and remains so despite everything. To quote Michael again:

> 'Just like it's hard for the government to convince all Australians that it planned well ahead of this fire crisis, it's difficult to for all of us to see an effective plan to reduce Australia's carbon emissions. The Morrison Government has announced a Royal Commission into the fires, at the same time as it's relying on accounting tricks to meet this country's agreements in the Kyoto Protocol. It appears there is no plan to tackle either issue, just strategies to minimise our efforts to change on both fronts.'

Yet like so many other issues – and this goes not just for Australia but other countries like the US as well – the people and their leaders don't always see eye to eye.

Australia's statistics don't include the possible thousands of inhabitants living off-grid. And a lot of effort on the part of individuals is going into finding weird and wondrous ways of harvesting water from the air, or the sun, or who knows what.

For the time being temperatures in Australia have dropped, rain has fallen in New South Wales and in Melbourne – which had its wettest January on record I believe – and hailstorms the size of tennis balls have battered Canberra, smashing cars, roofs, trees and a series of greenhouses belonging to the CSIRO (The Commonwealth Scientific and Industrial Research Organisation), ruining several years of research work.[9] Much of the rain has collected dust particles in the air and falls as mud. Dust storms have enveloped country towns, falling ash has poisoned rivers and killed thousands of fish. At the same time torrential rain has put out most of the fires, and now firefighters are hard at work coping with floods. Tourists – local and international – could not cancel their holidays fast enough.

But now the whole world knows a good deal more about Australia than it ever did in my living memory. Maybe with the world's eyes on them the powers that be may start to look at things differently. Or just maybe, once the fuss has died down, along with the fires – though since February is still full summer in Australia it doesn't pay to be complacent – the world will forget all about Australia and life will just go on as before.

That's if Australians will allow it.

Afterword

If you have enjoyed this book it would mean a great deal to me if you could post a review on Amazon.

And of course if you have not already done so, you might like to take a look at my two books on Australia based on my family history:

The Worst Country In The World (published 2012)
A Country To Be Reckoned With (published 2018)

Author biography

Patsy Trench was born in England to an Australian mother and Anglo-Irish father. She began her working life as an actress, in the UK and in Australia, where highlights were performing alongside local legends Chips Rafferty and Skippy the Bush Kangaroo (not at the same time). She has been a scriptwriter, script editor, playscout and lyricist, and co-founder of The Children's Musical Theatre of London, creating devised musicals shows with primary school-aged children.

She is the mother of two adult children and lives in London with a Freedom Pass. When not writing books she organises theatre tours and teaches theatre part-time at Kingston University to visiting students from overseas.

Her hobbies are rag-rugging and fossicking for ancient artefacts on the Thames foreshore.

She can be found at:

Facebook: PatsyTrenchWriting
Twitter: @PatsyTrench
Instagram: claudiafaraday1920
Website: www.patsytrench.com

Bibliography

<u>Books</u>

Booth, Douglas, *Australian Beach Cultures,* London, Frank Cass, 2001

Bryson, Bill, *Down Under,* London, Doubleday, 2000

Chatwin, Bruce, *Songlines*, London, Jonathan Cape, 1987

Clarke, James Stanier and McArthur, John, *The Life of Admiral Lord Nelson, K.B., from His Lordship's Manuscripts*, Vol 1 p15

Dillon, Patrick, *Concrete Reality, Denys Lasdun and the National Theatre*, London, National Theatre 2015

Fairfax, John, & Sons, *The Sydney Morning Herald and its Record of Australian Life 1831-1931*
 https://archive.org/details/b1047054/page/n13

Farwell, George, *Squatter's Castle*: *the life of Edward Ogilvie,* New South Wales, Harper Collins, 1973

Gledhill, PW, *Manly and Pittwater, its beauty and progress*, Manly, Warringah and Pittwater Historical Society, 1948

Grenville, Kate, *The Secret River*, Melbourne, Canongate, 2005

Huntsman, Leone, *Sand In Our Souls*, Melbourne University Press, 2001

Lawrence, DH, *Kangaroo*, Hastings, Delphi Classics, 2019

(Originally published London, Martin Secker, 1923)

Matcham, Mary Eyre, *The Nelsons of Burnham Thorpe*, London, John Lane, The Bodley Head, 1911

Messent, David, *Opera House Act One*, Melbourne, 1997

Michie, Archibald, *Going Circuit at the Antipodes*, published in *Household Words*, Vol IV, conducted by Charles Dickens, New York, Angell, Engel & Hewitt, 1852

Murray, Peter, *The Saga of Sydney Opera House*, Sydney, Spon Press, 2004

Russell, Ebert, *Australia's Amphibians*, Lone Hand, 1910

Starck, Nigel, *The First Celebrity, Anthony Trollope's Australasian Odyssey*, South Australia, Writes of Passage, 2014

Tomalin, Claire, *Charles Dickens, A Life*, London, Viking, 2011

Trench, Patsy, *The Worst Country in the World*, London, Prefab Publications, 2012

Trench, Patsy, *A Country To Be Reckoned With*, London, Prefab Publications, 2018

Trollope, Anthony, *Australia and New Zealand*, Vol 1, Leipzig, Bernhardt Tauchnitz, 1873

Twain, Mark, *The Wayward Tourist*, Melbourne University Press, 2006. Foreword by Don Watson

Williams, Kate, *England's Mistress: The Infamous Life of Emma Hamilton*, London, Hutchinson, 2006.

Newspapers, Journals and Pamphlets

Capper, Henry, *The Australian Colonies: where they are, and how to get to them,* Broombridge & Sons, London, 1855

Lansbury, Coral, JRAHS, Vol 52 part 2, 1966

Price, Richard, *The Paris Review Interviews*, Vol 1, Picador 2007

ABC News

Australian Star

Evening News

Sydney Morning Herald
Sydney Sportsman
Sunday Sun
The New European

Plays and films
Rattigan, Terence, *A Bequest to the Nation,* 1973
The Nelson Affair, 1973

Online
John Clarke: https://mrjohnclarke.com/projects/the-games
Countryeconomy.com:
    https://countryeconomy.com/countries/compare/austra
    lia/euro-zone
Daily Telegraph:
    https://www.telegraph.co.uk/news/uknews/6451152/Lo
    rd-Nelson-returned-to-work-half-an-hour-after-losing-
    arm.html
Emma Hamilton Society:
    http://www.emmahamiltonsociety.co.uk/grover-talk-
    2.html
engineering-timelines.com:
    http://www.engineering-timelines.com/who/
    arupOve10.asp
The Guardian:
    https://www.theguardian.com/lifeandstyle/2017/jan/14/
    children-family-histories-tales
The Guardian:
    https://www.theguardian.com/stage/theatreblog/2010/o
    ct/28/name-donation-dorfman-cottesloe
Inside History: https://insidestory.org.au/dh-lawrences-
    australian-experiment/
Museum of Old and New Art:
    https://mona.net.au/museum

UN Human Development Reports:
https://www.hdr.undp.org/en/2018-update
World Atlas: https://www.worldatlas.com/articles/the-best-countries-to-live-in-the-world.html
Worldometers.info:
https://www.worldometers.info/world-population/europe-population/

Footnotes

Prologue
[1] The miraculous online archive of Australian newspapers.

Chapter 1
[1] https://www.theguardian.com/lifeandstyle/2017/jan/14/children-family-histories-tales

[2] At the time of my migration I was working as an actress, hardly an undersubscribed profession. But it didn't seem to matter then.

[3] http://www.hdr.undp.org/en/2018-update. However according to other surveys such as Worldatlas.com, which measures 'education, job security, economic prosperity, and healthcare', Australia doesn't even make it into the top ten.

[4] Since first writing this our government has taken an alarming lurch to the right. Hopefully by the time you read this we will have managed to rid ourselves of it.

[5] https://mrjohnclarke.com/projects/the-games, cited on *Wikipedia*.

Chapter 3
[1] Martin is not his real name as I have not asked his permission to use it.

[2] Committee on Land Bill, Notes and Proceedings, Legislative Council 1839.

[3] William Ogilvie and George Wyndham, cited in *Squatter's Castle: the life of Edward Ogilvie* by George Farwell. Broadly speaking a Gymnosophist is someone who eschews creature comforts in favour of meditation.

[4] *The Life of Admiral Lord Nelson, K.B.,* from *His Lordship's Manuscripts* by *James Stanier Clarke and John McArthur, vol. i. p. 15.* (Cited in *The Nelsons of Burnham Thorpe*)

[5] https://www.telegraph.co.uk/news/uknews/6451152/ Lord-Nelson-returned-to-work-half-an-hour-after-losing-arm.html By Alastair Jamieson, 28 Oct 2009 [accessed 26/3/2019]. According to this report Nelson lost his eye at the Battle of the Nile in 1798, which is incorrect, proving you can never quite trust what you read in the newspapers.

[6] Moreen is a heavy cotton fabric.

[7] From *England's Mistress: The Infamous Life of Emma Hamilton* by Kate Williams.

[8] From a talk given by Alex Grover, Assistant Curator at the Royal Museums Greenwich, on 27/2/2019. http://www.emmahamiltonsociety.co.uk/grover-talk-2.html

Chapter 5

[1] Coral Lansbury, JRAHS, Vol 52 part 2, 1966

[2] Cited in *The First Celebrity, Anthony Trollope's Australasian Odyssey* by Nigel Starck

[3] *Australia and New Zealand*, Vol 1, by Anthony Trollope

[4] *The First Celebrity*, p12

[5] *Australia & New Zealand,* Vol 1, chap 4, pp64-76

[6] *Australia & New Zealand,* chap 7, pp117-8

[7] Walter Murdoch, prof of English at UWA in *Home Truths for Australia*, in 1938, cited in Starck.

[8] Don Watson, in the Introduction to *The Wayward Tourist* by Mark Twain

[9] https://insidestory.org.au/dh-lawrences-australian-experiment/ Susan Lever, 21 October 2015.

[10] Taken from Paul Daley, *The Guardian*, 16/10/17 [accessed 24/9/19] https://www.theguardian.com/australia-news/postcolonial-blog/2017/oct/16/travel-and-endless-talk-connected-me-to-details-chatwins-songlines-missed

[11] Cited in *The Guardian,* Stephen Moss, 5 July 2000 https://www.theguardian.com/books/2000/jul/05/billbryson

[12] Cited in *The First Celebrity*.

Chapter 6

[1] *Australian Beach Cultures* by Douglas Booth

[2] *Australian Beach Cultures*

[3] *Sand in Our Souls* by Leone Huntsman

[4] *Australian Beach Cultures*

[5] *Sydney Morning Herald*, 15 Oct 1907, cited in *Sand in our Souls*

[6] *Australian Star,* 21 October 1907, p5. This lad was I think a professional entertainer hired especially for the occasion.

[7] *Sydney Sportsman*, 23 October 1907, p4

[8] *Evening News,* 15 October 1907, p6

[9] *Evening News,* 12 October 1907, p8

[10] *Sunday Sun,* 23 September 1945, cited in *Sand in Our Souls.*

[11] *Sydney Morning Herald*, 23 December 1956, cited in *Sand in our Souls.*

[12] Dr Bowker, an eminent sportsman, interviewed about the skirt controversy in *The Evening News*, 14 October 1907, p6.

[13] *Evening News,* 15 October 1907, p6.

[14] *The Sydney Morning Herald and its Record of Australian Life 1831-1931* (John Fairfax & Sons, pp406-7) https://archive.org/details/b1047054/page/n13

[15] *Australia's Amphibians* by Ebert Russell

[16] *Sand In Our Souls*

[17] *Sydney Morning Herald,* 13 February 1999. (Cited in Booth)

Chapter 7

[1] https://countryeconomy.com/countries [Accessed 30/5/2019]

[2] https://www.worldometers.info/world-population/europe-population/ [Accessed 30/5/2019]

[3] https://mona.net.au/museum

Chapter 8

[1] *The Saga of Sydney Opera House* by Peter Murray

[2] *The Saga of Sydney Opera House*

[3] http://www.engineering-timelines.com/who/arup_O/arupOve10.asp

[4] *Act One* by David Messent

[5] *Act One*

[6] *The Saga of Sydney Opera House*
[7] Elizabeth Farrelly (Wikipedia)
[8] *The Saga of Sydney Opera House*
[9] *Utzon and the Sydney Opera House,* by E. Duek Cohen, A Review by Graham Pont
[10] ABC News 7 October 2018

Chapter 9

[1] *Concrete Reality, Denys Lasdun and the National Theatre* by Patrick Dillon. Dillon was the architect in charge of the refurbishment of the building in 2015.
[2] *Concrete Reality*
[3] *The Guardian,* 20 October 2010, https://www.theguardian.com/stage/theatreblog/2010/oct/28/name-donation-dorfman-cottesloe [Accessed 20/9/2019]
[4] Under Ted Heath, in 1974, coalminers went on strike, so in order to conserve fuel the country went on a 'three-day week', where electricity was restricted for all but essential services to three days in the week.

Chapter 10

[1] Tim Walker, *The New European*, 6 September 2019

Postscript

[1] The title of my first book about my family history in Oz.
[2] https://www.bbc.co.uk/news/world-australia-50951043
[3] One of whom was described as a 'grandmother'. Why this was deemed a relevant description of a 60-something-year old, with the possible implication that she was too old and frail – and maybe even stupid – not to be able to save herself is a moot point. (She was none of these things by all accounts.)
[4] https://www.abc.net.au/news/2019-11-14/nsw-bushfires-inside-small-town-wiped-out-wytaliba/11702106
[5] The rest is made up of oil and gas. 75% of energy generated in Australia comes from coal. I don't understand what happens to the 35% that isn't consumed. https://www.ga.gov.au/scientific-topics/energy/basics

[6] The rest comes from natural gas 41% and 21% nuclear. https://www.energy-uk.org.uk/our-work/generation/electricity-generation.html

[7] According to Claire O'Neill, who was sacked from her position organising a UN climate change conference in Glasgow later in 2020.

[8] https://www.clickenergy.com.au/news-blog/12-countries-leading-the-way-in-renewable-energy/ There's some variation in percentages between online sources but the country rankings are much the same.

[9] https://www.theguardian.com/weather/2020/jan/21/ canberras-destructive-hailstorm-wipes-out-years-of-csiro-research

Printed in Great Britain
by Amazon

64173037R00073